Direct Marketing Quantified

The Knowledge is in the Numbers

Gary Hennerberg

From the editors of:

Philadelphia, PA

From the editors of:

Direct Marketing Quantified
The Knowledge is in the Numbers

COPYRIGHT © 2005 Gary Hennerberg

ISBN: 1-931068-22-4

Target Marketing Group Publications
1500 Spring Garden St., Ste. 1200
Philadelphia PA 19130

To arrange bulk purchases of this book for educational purposes, please contact the publisher.

To my wife, LoCinda, and daughters, Amy and Liza,
who supported my writing of this book.

It meant precious weekends spent away from them,
but through it all, they kept encouraging me.

Acknowledgements

There are many people who have inspired me to master the application of the numbers in direct marketing.

There are a few people, in particular, who have been instrumental in the creation of this book that I would like to acknowledge.

The design, art direction, and typesetting for this book—including the devices that help make the spreadsheets and charts easy to follow, interesting, and compelling—came from the design genius of Perry Steinhoff. Perry is a long-time friend, colleague, and creative alter ego. In addition to his graphical treatment that makes the book more comprehensible, he was instrumental in editing its content. Perry and I partner together on creative work for many direct marketing companies, and our work is often tested against control packages. We often outperform—dare I say, trounce—control packages through product and creative repositioning that can only come from the combination of exceptional copy and design that puts the customer first. You can learn more about Perry at vitalclarity.com.

Checking my theories, spreadsheets, and the accuracy of my assumptions was undertaken by one of the few people in this business whom I had the confidence would understand everything I wrote. Peter Spaulder could have written this book. He's now retired after decades of distinguished work in direct marketing as a marketer and consultant. Peter edited copy, challenged my approach, and made the content of this book better.

Other direct marketing professionals who read and gave constructive feedback on early drafts of this book include Steve Hawkins of Assurity Life Insurance Company, Robert Means of Collin Street Bakery, Rachel Mercer of American List Counsel, Laura McClendon of AllMedia, and Tom Stoker of Stoker Resources Group.

I would like to thank Target Marketing Group Publications and this book's editor, Hallie Mummert. A discussion with her, Target Marketing's Peggy Hatch, and Denny Hatch, at a Direct Marketing Association conference, gave life to the idea for this book. Their support and patience was much appreciated.

Finally, to you, the reader, I say thanks for reading my book and considering my approach to analyzing, measuring, and improving the profitability of direct marketing programs. This is an interconnected collection of tested and proven techniques that work. I wish you all the best.

Gary Hennerberg

About the Author

Gary Hennerberg has dedicated his career to the science and art of direct marketing. A scholarship from the Direct Marketing Educational Foundation to attend a Collegiate Institute in 1978 launched his direct marketing career. He studied to become a writer, but early in his career he recognized that understanding analytics would be a key to his success in direct marketing. For over a dozen years, he worked as a product manager and marketing manager at leading direct marketing companies. In 1992, he launched his analytic and creative consultancy, Hennerberg Group, Inc.

Hennerberg has worked with over 100 consumer, business-to-business, agricultural, and non-profit organizations and has successfully managed profitable and award-winning direct mail, catalogs, print ads, and inserts. He has worked with categories such as food, insurance, credit card marketing, magazine subscriptions, apparel, photofinishing, travel, home mortgages, non-profit, publishing, collectibles, jewelry, telecommunications, and more.

In addition to being an in-demand analytic consultant, today Hennerberg's work reaches back to his original career roots as a writer. He is now sought after as one of America's most successful direct mail advertising, catalog, and print copywriters. Hennerberg's tests often outperform control packages, and on more than one occasion his repositioning of products and creative concepts has beat control creative by over 50 percent. He believes it is his understanding of "the numbers" that enables him to master the direct marketing synergy pyramid—lists, offers, and creative—and devise strategies to take direct marketing programs to new levels of profitability.

He has published many articles and is a speaker at direct marketing conferences and seminars. More information about Gary Hennerberg can be found at hennerberg.com.

Since 1993, Gary has been a performer with The Vocal Majority® Chorus, America's Premier Pops Chorus, based in Dallas. He sings bass and also has served as the organization's vice president of marketing.

He welcomes feedback about *Direct Marketing Quantified* by email: *gary@hennerberg.com.*

Contents

The Knowledge is in the Numbers

Introduction

The secret kept by successful direct marketers is that they have mastered how to analyze and interpret their marketing numbers to maximize profitability.

There are many approaches to analyzing data. Those described in this book have worked for many direct marketing companies. As you read my methodologies, you may find your experience has been similar. Or, you may disagree with my analytic thinking. That doesn't necessarily mean that one way is right and the other is wrong; it simply reinforces the premise that analysis can be achieved in different ways.

Knowing your numbers often drives your marketing strategy.

In this book, you'll learn proven analytic tools that have made money. As my direct marketing career has evolved, so has my need to learn how to better analyze and interpret the numbers. I have successfully analyzed and measured client direct marketing programs using these techniques. In some instances, there were prototypes of models to follow. In most situations, I used my imagination to devise a model that would yield vital knowledge that would mold strategy and tactical steps.

Every organization has a unique set of goals. Some organizations want to make money quickly, so you need to know exactly what a marketing initiative must do to breakeven by a certain time. Knowing when to breakeven often drives marketing strategy.

These methodologies apply to consumer and b-to-b marketers, fund raising, non-profit, catalog, and continuity marketers.

Some organizations may be in a profit cycle where they can afford to prospect more deeply into outside mailing lists and lose money on the initial acquisition. Those organizations are willing to bring on new customers at a higher loss because they want to ensure they have active customers at a future date.

Other uses for the numbers tend to be more tactical in nature and essential to run day-to-day operations. It's useful, for example, to be able to project a final response rate based on early response. You'll want to know how to evaluate test results to determine if a test package confidently beat your control. You may want to use a ZIP code model to lift response from under-performing lists. You may want to segment your customers into categories, based on sales. Customer segmentation will reveal which customers you should concentrate your marketing efforts on versus customers you may be surprised to find you should ignore.

The models in this book will benefit many types of organizations and media. The methodology applies to a consumer marketer and business-to-business marketer alike. It applies to fund-raising organizations and non-profits. It also works for catalog marketers and continuity, or club, marketers.

The models can be applied to a wide variety of media. However, the focus in this book is on direct mail and catalogs since postal mail is by far the largest medium used by direct marketing companies. But the principles hold true for other media such as e-mail, print, broadcast, inserts, and insert media.

Years ago, I created a "Measurable Marketing I.Q. Test," first published in *Target Marketing Magazine* in 1993. Now, more than a decade later, I have gone back to those questions and found that only a few modifications are needed. The questions are fundamental, yet knowing the answers establishes the foundation for a successful direct marketing organization.

As you read the updated "Direct Marketing Quantified I.Q. Test," below, answer each question simply "Yes" or "No" by circling the Y or N, and track the number of times you were able to confidently answer "Yes." Unless you can be confident in your answer, you should be fair to yourself and your organization and answer "No."

Y N 1. Do you know the average sale (in dollars) from a first-time buyer?

Y N 2. Do you know how many times an average customer purchases from you during a one-year period?

Y N 3. Do you know the percentage rate of retention of first-time buyers versus multiple-time buyers?

Y N 4. Do you know the sales value of an average customer after one year?

Y N 5. Do you know the value of sales within the past year from your top 20 percent of customers?

Y N 6. Do you know the required response and conversion levels your marketing programs must deliver to meet your profit objectives?

Y N 7. Do you base decisions about the success of marketing programs on the long-term sales value of your customer?

Can you confidently answer "yes" to at least 10 of these questions?

Y N 8. Have you included all product or service fulfillment costs in your profitability calculations?

Y N 9. Do you allocate sales from unknown order sources to get a better view of how all marketing programs are performing?

Y N 10. Do you create circulation plans based on list performance that includes the effect of cumulative sales and circulation, along with an allocation of sales from unknown sales sources?

Y N 11. Do you use ZIP code models to lift response rates to help under-performing outside lists become more profitable?

Y N 12. Do you have a response projection model in place that helps you read early results so you can accurately forecast final response rates?

Y N 13. Do you read your test results using statistical confidence intervals so you can be certain that your test program really beat your control package?

Y N 14. If you are a catalog marketer, do you use square-inch analysis to drive decisions about future space allocation and catalog pagination?

Using estimates — without real data — can be costly

So, how did you do? Were you able to confidently answer "Yes" to at least 10 of these questions? You should. You may be able to quickly look up the answer somewhere or have an estimate for what the answer should be. But your best estimate of an important metric may be off enough to perilously alter your marketing strategies and the ultimate profitability of your marketing program.

Today's most profitable organizations are those that routinely analyze marketing programs and use many of these tools to be more profitable. The days of being able to guess the performance of your marketing programs are long gone. The rapidly changing, competitive marketplace will eliminate those who don't thoroughly evaluate their businesses.

Using the measurement tools described in this book will move you closer to stronger profitability. And whether you agree with the methodology described in this book or not, the goal is to stimulate your thinking and make your direct marketing initiatives more profitable.

Gary Hennerberg

Chapter Synopsis

The chapters in this book follow a natural progression of phases that cycle through specific steps that quantify your direct marketing program.

The first phase — encompassing three chapters — will enable you to establish your course. The second phase (four chapters) reveals how to establish your goals for measurement. The third phase (three chapters) demonstrates how to measure your effectiveness. The final phase (four chapters) gives you optional extra tools to help you better quantify your marketing program.

Following the Chapter Synopsis is a graphic that illustrates the relationship between the four phases and each individual chapter. The graphic illustrates the importance of staying with the cycle and also indicates steps — or chapters — you may be able to skip.

Phase 1: Establishing Your Course

1. **Marketing Portfolio Management**

   Sets the stage for the importance of marketing to provide a reasonable Return on Investment (ROI) and lays the groundwork for understanding low, medium, and high risk marketing investments.

2. **Allocating Your Sales Dollar**

   Establishes cost categories and profit a sales dollar must cover: cost of goods sold (COGS), fulfillment, overhead, marketing, and contribution to profit. Marketing expense definitions and considerations for how you look at marketing costs are outlined.

3. **Defining and Establishing Breakeven Tolerance**

   Defines four ways to view breakeven; guidelines for what length of time you should define as an acceptable point to breakeven.

Phase 2: Setting the Bar

4. **Allowable Marketing Cost**

   How to establish what response rate must be achieved to meet profit objectives if you must make money from your first sale.

5. **Lead Generation Allowable Marketing Cost**

   Understanding the response rate you must achieve when using a two-step marketing program to first generate leads and convert those leads in the second step. Also described is a step-by-step allowable marketing cost guide for use when developing a lead generation program for sales people.

6. Forecasting Long-Term Sales

An essential model to create if you bring new customers on at a loss and expect those customers will become profitable at a future date.

7. Forecasting Future Breakeven

How to use your Long-Term Sales model to project at what future customer contact you will breakeven.

Phase 3: Measuring Effectiveness

8. Allocating Orders from Unknown Sources

Virtually every marketer has orders from unknown sources. This chapter explains how to allocate unassigned orders back to marketing programs for more comprehensive analysis.

9. Drawing Lines in the Sand of Circulation Analysis

How to "draw the line" in prospecting circulation analysis when using weighted averages of cumulative sales, cumulative circulation and an allocation of unknown orders. This chapter reveals how you can determine the exact depth you can mail into rented lists without compromising profitability.

10. ZIP Code Model Process and Methodology

After you have determined where to draw the line in your circulation plan, this chapter tells you how you can create a ZIP code model and apply it to lift response to under-performing lists, moving those lists "above the line" so you can mail them and achieve your profit goals.

Phase 4: Optional Extra Tools

11. Building Response Projection Curves

A step-by-step guide to building a model that projects response rates based on the number of days after a program has been mailed. It also explains how to determine the date that is the midpoint in your response curve.

12. Reading Test Results With Confidence

A description of how to use statistical confidence intervals to compare test results against each other and reliably know if the "winning" package beat another package. This chapter provides the formulas to calculate confidence intervals.

13. Customer Segmentation and Analysis

Does the Pareto Principle rule — that 80 percent of your profits come from 20 percent of your customers — apply to your business? Learn how to segment customers into deciles and quintiles to determine which customers are most important to you.

14. Square-Inch Analysis

Bonus chapter for catalog marketers: The hows and whys of developing an effective square-inch analysis for catalogs and multi-product brochures. Use this information to allocate space for your next catalog as well as to help paginate your catalog for better profitability.

15. Taking Action

Final reflections on taking action to use these tools to devise and execute profitable direct marketing initiatives.

The following flow chart, the "Hennerberg Analytic Cycle," helps bring context to each chapter, and serves as a road map through this book.

The Hennerberg Analytic Cycle

This flow chart represents the progression and relationships of the principals detailed in this book. The responsible Marketing Portfolio Manager never stops moving through the cycle, continually gathering more data, refining offers, initiating further testing, improving response rates.

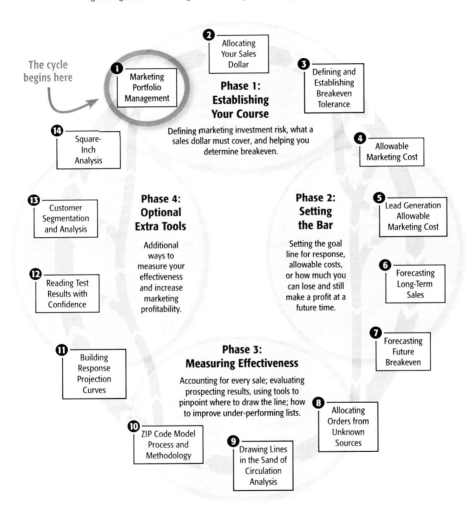

The cycle begins here

1 Marketing Portfolio Management

2 Allocating Your Sales Dollar

Phase 1: Establishing Your Course

Defining marketing investment risk, what a sales dollar must cover, and helping you determine breakeven.

3 Defining and Establishing Breakeven Tolerance

4 Allowable Marketing Cost

14 Square-Inch Analysis

Phase 4: Optional Extra Tools

Additional ways to measure your effectiveness and increase marketing profitability.

Phase 2: Setting the Bar

Setting the goal line for response, allowable costs, or how much you can lose and still make a profit at a future time.

5 Lead Generation Allowable Marketing Cost

13 Customer Segmentation and Analysis

12 Reading Test Results with Confidence

6 Forecasting Long-Term Sales

11 Building Response Projection Curves

Phase 3: Measuring Effectiveness

Accounting for every sale; evaluating prospecting results, using tools to pinpoint where to draw the line; how to improve under-performing lists.

7 Forecasting Future Breakeven

8 Allocating Orders from Unknown Sources

10 ZIP Code Model Process and Methodology

9 Drawing Lines in the Sand of Circulation Analysis

Chapter 1

Marketing Portfolio Management

Successfully managing your direct marketing program is much like the process of managing a stock portfolio—you research the possibilities, invest in the best prospects, analyze their performance, shed the under-performers, leverage what you've learned, and refine your strategy with the winners.

If you're a direct marketer, think of yourself as a Direct Marketing Mutual Fund Portfolio Manager. Every time you advertise and every year you're in business, the investors who own your organization will see the amount of money you have made from marketing investment dollars.

In many instances, as a direct marketer, you take greater risks than someone who is employed by a financial institution investing in a company's stocks. Think about it: When a direct marketing company generates $100 in sales, those dollars must cover fixed and variable costs. Consider the two scenarios in Illustration 1.1 (next page).

Depending upon your cost structure, about $35 to $60 of your sales dollars will have to cover cost of goods sold (COGS). Another $8 to $25 will have to cover fulfillment of the product. Another $7 to $12 must cover overhead. At each extreme, that leaves $3 to $50 as a contribution toward marketing expense and profit. If you spent $25 to generate $100 in sales, depending upon your fixed and variable costs, you either have a deficit of $22 or a profit of $25. That's a wide range. And it's the difference between being in business tomorrow and closing.

Illustration 1.1

	Scenario 1: PROFIT	Scenario 2: LOSS
Sales	$100	$100
Cost of Goods Sold (COGS)	$35	$60
Fulfillment	$8	$25
Overhead	$7	$12
Contribution to Marketing and Profit	$50	$3
Marketing	$25	$25
Profit (Loss)	$25	($22)

If your costs were too high and you lost $22, you're either going to have to borrow money or someone doesn't get paid.

But if you spent $25, generated $100 in sales, paid back the $25 in marketing costs, covered COGS, fulfillment and overhead, and had $25 remaining, your ROI from the initial $25 marketing cost is $25, or 100 percent. You've doubled your marketing investment in a short period of time. If you have achieved that, you've likely done better than most Wall Street mutual fund managers who manage millions of investor dollars.

Three Direct Marketing Components

What does it take for your marketing initiative, using the previous example, to generate a $25 profit versus a $22 loss? The fact of the matter is that losing $22 may be acceptable because you'll make that money back in the future (more about that in chapters 3, 6, and 7).

Managing Investment Risk

How do you manage risk for your marketing investment portfolio? You might characterize and rank your marketing program investments into categories such as low risk, medium risk, and high risk. The more historical data you have about a previous mailing or campaign, the greater your confidence in predicting the outcome of a repeat mailing. Thus, the less data you have, the higher the risk.

As an established company, for example, you might want to place 70 percent of your marketing dollars into low risk investments, 20 percent in medium risk investments, and 10 percent into high risk investments. Or maybe the goal for a calendar year focuses on expanding your customer file. If so, maybe you'll venture into a marketing risk posture of 50 percent low risk, 30 percent medium risk, and 20 percent high risk. Or at the other end of the spectrum, if it is a year to stabilize your profitability, you may prefer a ratio where 90 percent of marketing investments is low risk; 10 percent is medium risk, and you take no high risk marketing postures at all.

Like a financial investment manager, you should diversify your portfolio, depending on your organization's situation and goals.

If you are a new company, or new to using direct marketing, by definition most (and perhaps all) of your marketing will be high risk. There is simply no track record to measure against.

As you evaluate risk, keep in mind there are three direct marketing ingredients that must all come together for a successful program: media, offer, and creative. You can read more about how these three components come together to help you define risk in the related sidebar on page 18, titled *The Direct Marketing Synergy Pyramid*.

Low Risk Investments

Low risk investments are easy to spot. For an established company, it involves putting marketing dollars into what you know will provide an acceptable return on investment. With a few media choices, your low risk investments will look like this:

▶ **Direct Mail** — Proven creative, offers, and mailing lists that you use again and again.

▶ **Print** — Advertising in magazines, journals, newspapers or other print media where a proven track record of experience exists.

▶ **Insert Media** — Inserts, statement stuffers and other insert programs that are proven to return acceptable results for you.

▶ **Per Inquiry (PI)** — A low risk marketing program when payment to print, broadcast or insert media vehicles is based on the number of inquiries or orders generated. In this arrangement, you pay for the development of the creative, but instead of buying space or time, you pay for every inquiry or order generated.

▶ **Remnant Space** — Usually sold at very low rates in the days or hours before a print vehicle goes to press. If you can react quickly, and choose media whose demographics align well with those of your customers, you may view such marketing to be low risk because of the low cost.

Regarding broadcast: If you are buying air time, its dynamics put it into either medium or high risk investment. The three key components—media, offer, and creative—fatigue much faster in dynamic media, such as broadcast. Examples of media with higher fatigue potential (meaning the response rate to the marketing message dwindles quickly after only a few iterations, and so must constantly be freshened) include e-mail marketing, web search engine marketing, and broadcast (both infomercials and conventional paid advertising). A direct mail control package may be effective for months, perhaps years, whereas other media may fatigue after only a few days or weeks.

Low risk investments are predictable, but limit your opportunity to discover a big idea.

Remember, too, that low marketing cost probably equals low risk. So if you are testing something completely new but the cost is low, you may deem it a low risk.

Medium Risk Investments

A medium risk investment means that you have some, but not total, exposure to loss of your marketing investment and ROI. Medium risk investments look different than low risk. When you make a medium risk investment you need to keep in mind that the money you are investing may, in fact, represent a reduction to your marketing ROI. Therefore, you need to determine your tolerance for loss. Of course, taking a medium risk may have high rewards — which is the reason you are making modifications to your marketing initiatives to test if you can improve upon something you are already doing.

You might consider medium risk investments under these scenarios:

► **Direct Mail** — New creative combined with proven offers and mailing lists, or new lists combined with proven creative and offers, or a new offer combined with proven creative and lists, are illustrative of direct mail possibilities. In any case, this assumes you change only one of these three elements: list, offer or creative.

► **Web-Based Advertising** — Paid advertising with proven results but where web users turn over rapidly could be deemed medium risk.

► **Search Engine Marketing** — Ranking high on search engines enhances your visibility. Because costs can be low or even none for organic web search (when you rank high "organically" without buying the listing), search engine marketing may be considered medium risk. However, if your business strategy relies on being found on search engines to generate web site traffic, you are in a high risk category due to technology and search rules regularly being changed, without notice.

► **E-Mail Marketing** — Subject lines and messages based on tested and proven attributes could be medium risk, provided you comply with legislation relating to "spamming."

► **Print** — Another proven medium risk might involve advertising in magazines, journals, newspapers or other print media where you have a proven track record of experience, but where you are using new creative or offers. Or, you might use proven creative in new publications that mirror the types of readers with whom you have found success elsewhere.

► **Insert Media** — Inserts, statement stuffers and other insert programs where creative is proven but the audience is different; or, testing new creative in proven insert media you have used.

► **Broadcast** — When utilizing infomercials or 30- or 60-second ads, if you return to the same markets and advertise at the same time with a consistent message, you may consider this to be medium risk.

High Risk Investments

High risk investments are those in which you can't confidently predict your outcome, because you have little or no historical data to evaluate. You must be willing to lose all of your marketing dollars and not have enough sales to ever recover cost of goods sold (COGS), fulfillment, and overhead. If you are testing a new product, virtually all your marketing investment is going to be high risk (even if the product is an extension of an already successful product). If you're a new company, your marketing is probably high risk because you have no proven track record or brand trust.

High risk can be a big gamble, but it can yield a big payoff.

Exceptions

What if your business model limits itself to web-based or broadcast marketing? Are you destined to failure? Of course not. There are many successful enterprises that do not use direct mail, print, and insert media. Yet those web-based or broadcast-oriented companies perform well.

Clearly, it's possible to be profitable and use high risk marketing investments. But in those cases, the monitoring and evaluation of performance must be completed on a daily, if not hourly, basis. Frequent evaluation, and the ability to instantly pull the plug on unprofitable marketing, removes exposure from large losses using dynamic media.

The Direct Marketing Synergy Pyramid

There are three components that when properly combined yield direct marketing success: media, offers, and creative. For years, direct marketers have subscribed to the philosophy that 40 percent of your success comes from your mailing list, 40 percent is due to your offer, and 20 percent is due to your creative.

Here's a new take I've devised on an old concept. See if you don't agree that it's more reflective of today's direct marketing environment.

I have subscribed to that weighting percentage of importance myself. But I have modified my stance on this axiom based on a number of experiences in recent years. For one thing, direct marketing today is delivered through so many different promotional vehicles that the broader term "media" is more appropriate than "mailing list." Successful direct marketers often use multiple media to expand their markets. Broadcast is used to generate telephone calls. Catalogs, direct mail and e-mail are used to drive traffic to web sites. Insert media is used to acquire new customers. We market in a multi-dimensional media world.

With traditional U.S. Postal Service delivery of much of our marketing material via catalogs and direct mail, this media vehicle remains highly important to most direct marketers. Mailing lists and how they are compiled and enhanced have evolved over the years. Established direct marketers usually can, with great accuracy, predict response from a tested mailing list during a rollout. Once core lists have been identified, one of the strategic foundations is in place for future marketing.

The second strategic foundation is your offer. Your offer — that is, the price, what's included, what's free, what your customer will get — is the proposition that prompts a response. Testing new offers is essential, but once a control offer has been identified, it can take years to identify a break-through new offer that outperforms the control. In some cases, marketers have little flexibility in changing offers due to regulatory concerns, competition, or cost.

Together, the media and offers that have been established are a strong foundation upon which break-through creative can drive greater response rates.

For the synergy of the three primary direct marketing components — media, offer, and creative — I visualize them in a pyramid (see the illustration on page 21). As a pyramid, you can see how proven media and offers serve as the foundation. Both must be solidly in place to support the creative vehicle to sell your customer or prospect. When media and the offer are solid, it is the creative at the tip of the pyramid that can make a huge impact on your success.

Creative is, of course, a discipline unto itself. Sometimes it's thought of as only the obvious duo of copy and design. But more than that, it's the underlying way that a message is used to intrigue, convince, and motivate a human being to respond.

Part of that process is how the product is positioned. A big challenge is how to take an established product, well-known in the marketplace, and breathe new life into it. One approach might be to "reinvent" it through repositioning. Is it possible to rename, or recast an old product in a new light? Is there a story—romance about how the product is made, or a focus on the distinct benefits it delivers to a new demographic— that gives it a completely new appeal? As products mature, often the target audience ages, too. Eventually, the only people who purchase the product are of an older age. Replenishing older age customers with younger age customers is essential if your business is to sustain itself. But how do you do that if the product is perceived by younger customers as a relic of yesteryear? Repositioning the product is one way to succeed with your creative.

Your offer may also be a candidate for repositioning. What if you have a low introductory price that has become the standard in your industry and you have little flexibility to change it? Test repositioning it. Or reposition the price point so that instead of stating its price, such as "$25 a month," play up that it's less than what you spend daily for an everyday expenditure like a cup of coffee.

Of course, in direct mail your letter's headline must proclaim a big promise. The teaser and engaging design of your outer envelope can make a huge difference in response. Imagine what happens if you double the number of people who open your envelope—you double your odds of getting a response.

When the media and offer are proven, it's the creative you test that can provide extraordinary lift. Imagine what happens when you lift response by 50 percent or more through repositioning the product and using stronger creative to sell the product (an accomplishment I've both created and witnessed). What if your lift in response is only 25 percent? Or only 15 percent? Who wouldn't dream of those types of increases in response, sales, and ultimately profits?

That's why I place creative on the top of the pyramid, supported by the foundation of proven media and offers. The right creative—positioning, copy, and design—has great potential to deliver a quantum leap in direct marketing performance.

The Direct Marketing Synergy Pyramid

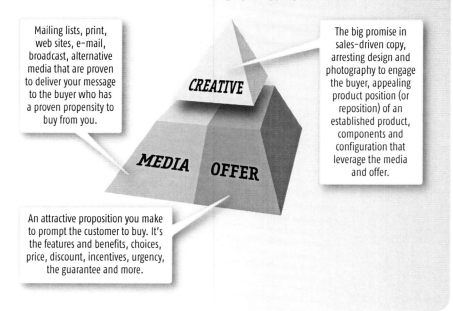

Mailing lists, print, web sites, e-mail, broadcast, alternative media that are proven to deliver your message to the buyer who has a proven propensity to buy from you.

The big promise in sales-driven copy, arresting design and photography to engage the buyer, appealing product position (or reposition) of an established product, components and configuration that leverage the media and offer.

CREATIVE

MEDIA OFFER

An attractive proposition you make to prompt the customer to buy. It's the features and benefits, choices, price, discount, incentives, urgency, the guarantee and more.

The Hennerberg Analytic Cycle

This flow chart represents the progression and relationships of the principals detailed in this book. The responsible Marketing Portfolio Manager never stops moving through the cycle, continually gathering more data, refining offers, initiating further testing, improving response rates.

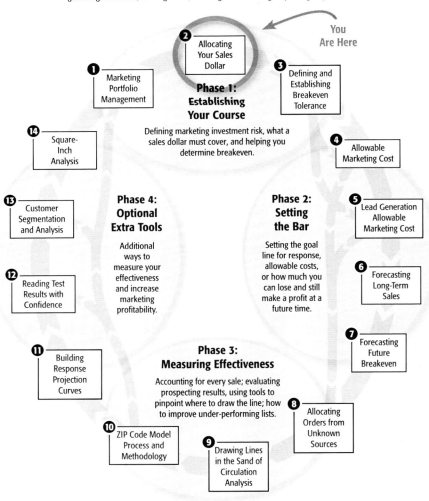

You Are Here

2 Allocating Your Sales Dollar

1 Marketing Portfolio Management

3 Defining and Establishing Breakeven Tolerance

Phase 1: Establishing Your Course

Defining marketing investment risk, what a sales dollar must cover, and helping you determine breakeven.

14 Square-Inch Analysis

4 Allowable Marketing Cost

Phase 4: Optional Extra Tools

Additional ways to measure your effectiveness and increase marketing profitability.

Phase 2: Setting the Bar

Setting the goal line for response, allowable costs, or how much you can lose and still make a profit at a future time.

13 Customer Segmentation and Analysis

5 Lead Generation Allowable Marketing Cost

12 Reading Test Results with Confidence

6 Forecasting Long-Term Sales

7 Forecasting Future Breakeven

11 Building Response Projection Curves

Phase 3: Measuring Effectiveness

Accounting for every sale; evaluating prospecting results, using tools to pinpoint where to draw the line; how to improve under-performing lists.

8 Allocating Orders from Unknown Sources

10 ZIP Code Model Process and Methodology

9 Drawing Lines in the Sand of Circulation Analysis

Chapter 2

Allocating Your Sales Dollar

Understanding how a sales dollar is allocated in a direct marketing business is critical. Every sales dollar must cover a cost and yield a contribution to profit.

Broadly speaking, every sales dollar should be allocated to cover five categories: cost of goods sold (COGS), fulfillment, overhead, marketing, and profit. One portion of your sales dollar will be allocated as profit contribution. Four portions are allocated as costs. Details about the numbers within these cost categories will be addressed later. For now, visualize a sales dollar and how percentages of it must be allocated. This illustration, 2.1, represents the way in which many direct marketing companies allocate their sales dollars. For example, 37 percent of the dollar will be used to pay COGS; 19 percent will be used to pay fulfillment; 6 percent will cover overhead; 26 percent will be invested in marketing; and 12 percent will remain for contribution to profit.

Illustration 2.1

COGS 37% | Fulfill-ment 19% | Over-head 6% | Marketing 26% | Profit Contri-bution 12%

Contribution to Marketing and Profit

Summary of Sales Dollar Categories

1. **Cost of Goods Sold (COGS)** – All costs related to your product or service. COGS typically range from 35 percent to 60 percent of a direct marketing company's sales dollar.

2. **Fulfillment** – All operational costs required to deliver your product or service to your customer. For most mature businesses, fulfillment expenses will range from 8 percent to 25 percent of your sales dollar.

3. **Overhead** – Salaries, rent, utilities, and other items that must be accounted for somewhere. Overhead generally runs from 5 percent to 12 percent for most mature businesses.

This is your area of responsibility, and knowing your numbers gives you the tools you need to manage it.

4. **Contribution to Profit and Marketing** – The amount remaining after COGS, fulfillment, and overhead are deducted from your sales dollar. These include:

   A. **Marketing** – All costs related to promoting your product. Most direct marketing businesses budget from 20 percent to 40 percent of their sales dollar for marketing costs.

   B. **Profit** – Money left over after all cost obligations have been paid.

It is important to understand the contribution to marketing and profit category. The marketing professional is responsible for managing that portion of the sales dollar. This is where you parallel the work of the investment manager for a mutual fund. Every dollar you spend on marketing must provide a return on investment.

Cost of Goods Sold

COGS usually are a fixed cost within a volume range assumption. These costs cannot be reduced unless you reduce your cost of production or costs from vendors. This brings an important point to the surface: you, or the people in charge of your product, must tightly negotiate costs. Every item that goes into the cost of an item should be analyzed. If you manufacture the product you sell, you need to understand if overhead directly related to manufacturing is allocated to COGS, or accounted for separately in the overhead category.

Fulfillment

Fulfillment also is usually a fixed cost within a volume range assumption. That being said, it is important that you negotiate the best rates possible from your shipper. Processing costs must be controlled, and if your business is seasonal, you must manage human resources as well. If you outsource fulfillment, make sure your costs are in line with market conditions.

There are other items that often fall into the fulfillment category. Among them:

▶ Shipping expense. If you charge shipping and handling, your sales dollars will be increased, and those dollars will be used to pay for the cost of fulfillment.

▶ Order processing costs

▶ Inbound telephone costs

▶ Order pick/packing

- ► Credit card fees
- ► Cost of giving free items (or premiums)
- ► Customer service (which alternatively might be placed in overhead)
- ► Bad debt
- ► Shrinkage for returned products

Either know the exact dollar amount for each of these items, or be prepared to use a percentage of sales. Some items will require that you allocate fulfillment costs based on weighted volume of orders. For example, if 60 percent of your orders are generated by inbound telephone, then the cost of inbound telephone calls should be charged toward only those 60 percent of your orders.

Overhead

Overhead usually is a fixed cost, but you can have a direct impact on overhead. Salaries increase as you add more people to payroll. If salaries are too high, reductions are unpleasant and can have long-term negative consequences if improperly managed.

Rent and utilities are other overhead costs that must be managed. Any additional uncategorized expenses should be allocated to overhead as well.

Beware Ego Overhead

From time to time, I have witnessed direct market-ing companies take on "ego overhead." This usually happens when there have been a couple of years of tremendous success and overhead inflates at such a degree that the owners and management forget that the odds exist that there will be lean years ahead. "Ego overhead" happens when the office space occupied is more opulent than is necessary. Some businesses require very nice offices because clients and customers visit. As a direct marketer, your clients or customers aren't likely to visit. Your office doesn't need to be conveniently located near a busy freeway. It doesn't need expansive marble lobbies. It doesn't need to be lavishly furnished with expensive desks and chairs. It doesn't need expensive artwork adorn-ing the walls. The most financially successful direct marketing companies I have seen do not take an "ego overhead" attitude.

If you're not head of the company, this will be a sticky wicket to approach. But it's the responsible thing to do.

Nevertheless, most of us enjoy working in nicely appointed offices. A nice environment is a more pleasant place to work. It helps recruit and retain good employees. It feels good. But there is a fine line between creating overhead that is truly productive and "ego overhead" that drains dollars from market-ing and profit.

Contribution to Marketing and Profit

After COGS, fulfillment, and overhead are deducted from your sales dollar, what's left must be used to cover marketing expenses and profit. Spend too much on marketing, and profit will suffer. Spend too little on marketing, and you won't generate enough volume of sales to cover your fixed costs. Balance it right, and you make smart marketing investments that meet your profit objectives.

Marketing Expenses

It's imperative that you monitor your marketing expenses. If you change your direct mail package and increase its cost by 5 percent, the change must justify itself by lifting response rates and sales to at least cover that cost.

Marketing expense comes in the form of:

- ▶ Creative costs paid to an agency or freelancer(s). If your creative is done in-house, that cost may be included in your overhead.

- ▶ Photography and pre-media (any prepress preparation for your printer)

- ▶ Printing

- ▶ Lettershop or direct mail insertion costs

- ▶ Postage

- ▶ List rental

- ▶ Space in print publications or insert media

- ▶ Broadcast time

- ▶ Creation, promotion, and maintenance of a web site

As you will read in the next chapters, the cost of marketing has a direct impact on profitability. Increasing marketing cost is acceptable as long as the response and profitability increases at least make up for the added cost.

Considerations When Calculating Marketing Costs

Sometimes there are special circumstances that alter how you look at or calculate your marketing expenses. Here are a few examples that may prompt you to allocate your marketing costs differently for direct mail or a catalog:

Carefully consider how you calculate your costs so you don't overburden — or underestimate — marketing expense.

1. If you mail to both your customer file and rented lists, separate the costs by list so list rental is not charged to customer costs.

2. Creative and development costs should be separated from mailing cost. Often these costs are built into a single promotional overhead number or budget. You may have exceptions, however, such as if the creative will be used only once or if you have expenses for changes that will be used only once.

3. When you print in small quantities for tests, be sure to evaluate performance based on projected costs for a rollout. If you're testing a quantity of 50,000 and expect to mail it to 500,000 if it's successful, base your evaluation of the program on the cost to produce 500,000, not 50,000. If you don't use the rollout cost, you'll bias your findings and your analysis will lead you to the wrong conclusion.

4. Some costs should be weighted to the percentage of orders. For example, if the percentage ratio of orders received by mail, web, and phone is 20%/20%/60%, the cost of BRE (Business Reply Envelope) postage should be charged for only 20 percent of the total orders, web maintenance should be charged to 20 percent of orders, and inbound phone costs should be charged to 60 percent of orders.

5. If you have surplus direct mail pieces that were not mailed, you should allocate all costs to what was actually mailed. However, if there is any chance you'll set those extras aside for later use, allocate the costs of the remaining circulation on the subsequent mail flights.

Key Response and Profit Measures

It's also helpful to understand the formulas for key metrics. Illustration 2.2 is an explanation of a number of these formulas. The first measurement in the table, response percent, may seem like a simple calculation (response divided by circulation times 100). However, it's easy to take the lazy step and mentally move the decimal point to arrive at the response rate, instead of multiplying by 100. But if you mentally move the decimal point just one digit off, your response rate will be either understated or overstated, by 10 times. This can be a very unforgiving error.

Illustration 2.2 provides a primer on calculations you should use for a variety of direct marketing measurements.

Illustration 2.2

Measurement	Definition
Response Percent	Responses ÷ mail quantity × 100
Average Order	Sales dollars ÷ number of orders
Sales Dollars per Thousand (Sales/M)	Sales dollars ÷ mail quantity in thousands
Marketing Cost per Thousand (Marketing Cost/M)	Marketing cost ÷ mail quantity in thousands
Marketing Cost Percent (%)	Marketing cost ÷ sales × 100
Profit per Thousand (Profit/M)	Profit dollars ÷ mail quantity in thousands
Profit Percent (%)	Profit dollars ÷ net sales × 100. Or, Profit/M ÷ Sales/M × 100
Profit per Buyer (Profit/Buyer)	Profit dollars ÷ number of buyers
Cost per Inquiry (Cost/Inquiry)	Marketing cost ÷ number of inquiries

The Case of the Wrong Decimal Point

A number of years ago a *Fortune 500* client asked me to sit in on a presentation being made by its advertising agency. The purpose was for me to provide my feedback on what the agency was proposing and double check the numbers. During the meeting, the agency account executive presented the results of a previous campaign showing the number of inquiries that had been generated. Using that number of inquiries, someone at the agency calculated the response rate, and that response rate was used to project response from an upcoming rollout into multiple magazines.

As I reviewed the numbers, I detected something amiss with the relationship of the inquiries and calculated response rate. Sure enough, whoever had prepared the presentation had failed to take the inquiries divided by circulation, then multiply that number by 100 to put the decimal point in its proper place and arrive at the percentage response rate. The error resulted in a stated response rate that was 10 times higher than the actual rate. As a result, the media buy recommendation was based on faulty data. It meant that the entire magazine rollout plan was flawed and would likely yield only one-tenth the response the client was led to believe it would generate.

The Hennerberg Analytic Cycle

This flow chart represents the progression and relationships of the principals detailed in this book. The responsible Marketing Portfolio Manager never stops moving through the cycle, continually gathering more data, refining offers, initiating further testing, improving response rates.

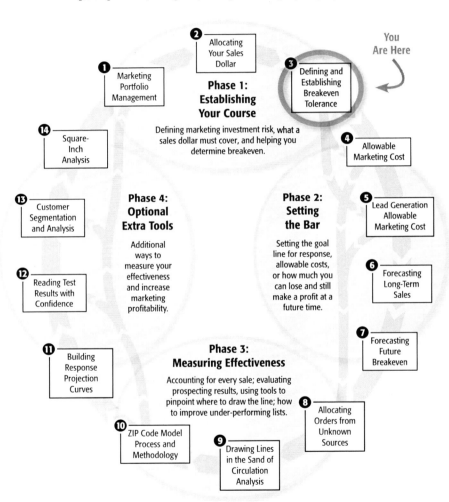

2 Allocating Your Sales Dollar

1 Marketing Portfolio Management

3 Defining and Establishing Breakeven Tolerance

You Are Here

Phase 1: Establishing Your Course

Defining marketing investment risk, what a sales dollar must cover, and helping you determine breakeven.

14 Square-Inch Analysis

4 Allowable Marketing Cost

13 Customer Segmentation and Analysis

Phase 4: Optional Extra Tools

Additional ways to measure your effectiveness and increase marketing profitability.

Phase 2: Setting the Bar

Setting the goal line for response, allowable costs, or how much you can lose and still make a profit at a future time.

5 Lead Generation Allowable Marketing Cost

12 Reading Test Results with Confidence

6 Forecasting Long-Term Sales

7 Forecasting Future Breakeven

11 Building Response Projection Curves

Phase 3: Measuring Effectiveness

Accounting for every sale; evaluating prospecting results, using tools to pinpoint where to draw the line; how to improve under-performing lists.

8 Allocating Orders from Unknown Sources

10 ZIP Code Model Process and Methodology

9 Drawing Lines in the Sand of Circulation Analysis

Chapter 3

Defining and Establishing Breakeven Tolerance

This chapter will help you determine the parameters you should establish to determine how to define breakeven for your organization and establish your tolerance for slower payback.

The previous chapter described how to allocate a sales dollar to cover five broad categories. The illustration showed the allocation of a sales dollar for cost of goods sold (COGS), fulfillment, overhead, and contribution to marketing and profit. COGS, fulfillment, and overhead are, for the most part, fixed. Marketing cost and profit are variable.

Spend more on marketing, and the percentage of the dollar intended for profit shrinks, or may even disappear. While prospecting for new customers, it is often accepted that there will be little, if any, portion of the dollar remaining for profit. In fact, new customers are usually brought on at a loss, hence the importance of determining your definition of breakeven and your acceptance of how far into the future it may be before you recover your costs. If you acquire new customers at a loss, one of two situations is present:

A. Your company is new, has a line of credit, and understands there won't be profit in its early stages, or,

B. You are an established company and your company's profits come from established customers.

There can be a point, however, where you overspend on marketing. When that happens, not only is there no profit, but you've spent money you don't have. That means either money must be borrowed, or someone doesn't get paid. Because of this, it is vital that you calculate your breakeven point so you don't drive your business into a negative cash situation.

Breakeven Definitions

Your definition of breakeven must be compatible with your organization's long-term financial objectives.

Breakeven requires definition, and sometimes it is altered to fit the circumstance. For the most part, there are four possible breakeven scenarios:

1. The minimum sales dollars needed to recover marketing, COGS, fulfillment, overhead, plus a targeted profit.

2. The minimum sales dollars needed to recover marketing, COGS, fulfillment, plus overhead. Profit is not required.

3. The minimum sales dollars needed to recover marketing, COGS, and fulfillment. Overhead would not be covered and profit is not required.

4. The minimum sales dollar loss you can tolerate on the first order to breakeven at a future date.

If you are prospecting for new customers, you need to determine which breakeven scenario is most acceptable to your organization. If your situation requires that you bring on new customers at a loss (the fourth scenario above), you are like many other direct marketing firms. Your organization will be in a vulnerable position, because are managing losses to acquire new customers. You will need to develop a Long-Term Sales Value model, which is discussed in Chapter 6, to help you manage those losses. If you must recover costs and make a profit on your first order, in Chapters 4 and 5 you will learn how to create Allowable Marketing Cost models.

Determining an Acceptable Breakeven Time Frame

How your organization defines breakeven is a decision that management and investors should make. If you are marketing to existing customers, you will likely view breakeven as option No. 1 above.

You also will opt for scenario No. 1 if you are prospecting for new customers and will sell to that customer only one time, requiring a profit on the first sale.

Your greatest flexibility to acquire the most new customers is when you can lose money on the initial acquisition, but know when you'll make it all back.

If you are prospecting for new customers and have the ability to sell to those customers again in the future, you may determine that options No. 2, No. 3 or No. 4 will work for your organization. At your most conservative, you would opt for option No. 2 (recovers all costs and overhead, but forgoes profit on the first sale). Option No. 3 gives you somewhat more flexibility, if you don't have to recover overhead or make a profit. But it's option No. 4 that offers the greatest flexibility toward breakeven. You will have the greatest growth potential if you view breakeven as the recovery of all costs during a repeat sale from a newly acquired customer at a future time.

If you are prospecting for new customers and losing money, there are a few contact parameters (defining frequency of contact) you must consider to determine the length of time acceptable before you breakeven. Here are a few possibilities:

Breakeven After 3 Contacts or 1 Year

Most direct marketers plan to sell to a newly acquired customer additional products or services. If you are using direct mail or a catalog and you mail to newly acquired customers throughout the year, you might determine that a new customer must become profitable after just three contacts. Some businesses will contact customers frequently; therefore, three contacts, if made on a monthly basis, will require breakeven in just three months. Some businesses are highly seasonal, so it's possible there may be only three contacts made during the course of one season (or year).

> *General Rule: If you require breakeven after three contacts, your overall universe of prospective customers will be smaller than if you can breakeven farther into the future.*

Breakeven after 6 Contacts or 2 Years

If you mail every 60 days, six contacts may constitute a one-year contact plan for new customers. If your business is seasonal and you only mail three times a year, this could stretch the length of breakeven time to two years.

> *General Rule: If you can wait six contacts for a return of your marketing investment, your universe and opportunity for more prospecting volume — or circulation — will be higher than for three contacts. But in all likelihood, your profitable universe of names will be only somewhat higher. The growth of your business will be faster than using three contacts, but it may not increase your mailing universe dramatically.*

Breakeven After 9 Contacts or 3 Years

This posture is for the marketer who understands that new customers are a long-term investment and that it will take time to yield profits. For some marketers, nine contacts may occur in a year or less. For others, three years may be required to go through nine contact cycles. It's more likely that this longer term position will be taken by a well-established marketer with many products to sell (probably in a catalog) who already has a high number of customers and a strong repeat purchase rate. A company with established and loyal customers is often in a position to fund new customer acquisition. Many established marketers assume it will take three years to breakeven. This position also may be reflected in organizations with patient investors who are taking the long-term view of building a direct marketing business.

> *General Rule: A nine-contact, or three-year, payback typically increases the universe of prospective customers considerably, permitting much faster growth of new customers.*

Ten or More Contacts/Four Year or More Breakeven

This position again increases the potential universe of customers much more dramatically, but this position brings with it a large risk. By the time you reach 10 contacts, which could be years into the future, the customers acquired earlier in your contact cycle may have changed their purchase habits. Repurchase from those customers may decline more quickly, resulting in the dangerous prospect of never breaking even from those customers.

Manage your optimism with realism, and be prepared to accept that there may be customers you acquired with whom you will never breakeven.

> *General Rule: Only mature businesses or those with deep pockets should take such a long view toward breakeven.*

The Hennerberg Analytic Cycle

This flow chart represents the progression and relationships of the principals detailed in this book. The responsible Marketing Portfolio Manager never stops moving through the cycle, continually gathering more data, refining offers, initiating further testing, improving response rates.

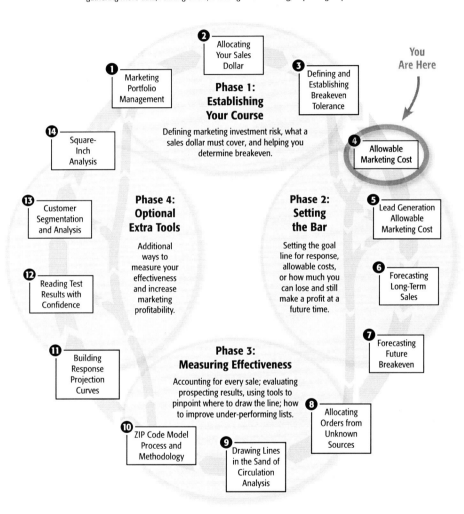

2 Allocating Your Sales Dollar

1 Marketing Portfolio Management

3 Defining and Establishing Breakeven Tolerance

You Are Here

Phase 1: Establishing Your Course

Defining marketing investment risk, what a sales dollar must cover, and helping you determine breakeven.

14 Square-Inch Analysis

4 Allowable Marketing Cost

13 Customer Segmentation and Analysis

Phase 4: Optional Extra Tools

Additional ways to measure your effectiveness and increase marketing profitability.

Phase 2: Setting the Bar

Setting the goal line for response, allowable costs, or how much you can lose and still make a profit at a future time.

5 Lead Generation Allowable Marketing Cost

12 Reading Test Results with Confidence

6 Forecasting Long-Term Sales

11 Building Response Projection Curves

7 Forecasting Future Breakeven

Phase 3: Measuring Effectiveness

Accounting for every sale; evaluating prospecting results, using tools to pinpoint where to draw the line; how to improve under-performing lists.

8 Allocating Orders from Unknown Sources

10 ZIP Code Model Process and Methodology

9 Drawing Lines in the Sand of Circulation Analysis

Chapter 4

Allowable Marketing Cost

There are two models you may choose from to help you determine response requirements if you must be profitable from your customer's first purchase. One is an Allowable Marketing Cost model, described in this chapter. A subset of the Allowable Marketing Cost model is a model for Lead Generation programs (described in Chapter 5).

The two models are similar, but they have different uses. The Allowable Marketing Cost illustration is useful if you are evaluating your profitability based on only one sale. If your business relies on making money (or breaking even, but not losing money) on the first sale from a new customer, this model—and chapter—is for you.

This chapter is particularly important if you must make a profit on your initial customer acquisition.

If you lose money on acquiring new customers, you need to develop a Long-Term Sales Value model described in Chapter 6. A Long-Term Sales Value model projects, over time, the point at which a new customer, who is initially brought on at a loss, will breakeven.

Chances are you don't need to create both an Allowable Marketing Cost model and a Long-Term Sales Value model. But you need one or the other to determine what level of response you need to generate from a new customer acquisition program. Review both chapters, and decide for yourself which approach makes more sense for your business.

Begin with First-Time Sale Value

You'll need to know the average order from a first-time customer. Include all dollars generated from this sale. If you charge shipping and handling (S&H), it should be listed as a separate revenue line item. The combined average order of a first-time customer and S&H will contribute toward gross sales (before returns or cancellations). If you charge sales tax, it should not be included in the model, since it is money collected that later will be remitted to the appropriate government agencies.

At the beginning of the model (Illustration 4.1), let's assume the average first-time order is $70.00 (Line 1). Shipping revenue is assumed at 10 percent of sales for this model; however, you likely will have an actual fixed amount that should be placed on Line 2.

If you're like most direct marketers, you'll have returns or refunds. For most companies, they may be minimal; for others, such as apparel, the returns can be high. Line 3 for this model assumes a return or refund rate of 2 percent. Line 4 provides us with our gross sales (product revenue plus shipping revenue less returns).

Illustration 4.1

A	B	C
Line	Item	Revenue
1	Average First-Time Product Sale	$70.00
2	Shipping Revenue (10% of Sales)	$7.00
3	Returns or Refunds (2% of Sales)	($1.40)
4	Gross Sales	$75.60

Cost of Goods Sold

Your cost of goods sold (COGS) should be straight-forward if you purchase your product from a vendor for an established price. If you manufacture your products, the calculation may be more challenging. However, it's likely your company's finance department already has calculated your COGS. As you research that number, be sure to know if other costs are included in your COGS, such as fulfillment and overhead. It's usually better to separate costs related to fulfillment and overhead in the event you have options to change them to help improve your outcome. If you don't have an exact dollar amount of COGS, use a percent of sales. This model assumes a percent of sales to determine COGS.

What follows, on this and the next 10 pages, is a step-by-step building of an Allowable Marketing Cost model, and how each step impacts the bottom line.

Continuing on with the development of the model, Illustration 4.2 incorporates cost of goods sold (Line 5) assumed to be 40 percent of sales. However, you'll see in Column F that COGS is 37 percent of the gross sales dollar after returns or refunds.

Illustration 4.2

A	B	C	D	E	F
Line	Item	Revenue			
1	Average First Time Product Sale	$70.00			
2	Shipping Revenue (10% of Sales)	$7.00			
3	Returns or Refunds (2% of Sales)	($1.40)			
4	**Gross Sales**	**$75.60**			
			Basis	Percent of Sales	COGS Per Sale	Percent Gross Sales
5	**Cost of Goods Sold**	$70.00	40%	$28.00	37%

Fulfillment

Costs that go into the fulfillment category are often the most detailed numbers to identify. Illustration 4.3, below, is an extension of sales and COGS. Here are several costs that should be considered for fulfillment costs. Your business circumstance may dictate additional or different costs that should be included.

Line 6 — Shrinkage. If some of your product must be replaced because it has been returned and cannot be sent to another customer, you must account for the loss of inventory. This model assumes 1 percent of sales are lost due to shrinkage.

Illustration 4.3

A	B	C
Line	**Item**	**Revenue**
1	Average First Time Product Sale	$70.00
2	Shipping Revenue (10% of Sales)	$7.00
3	Returns or Refunds (2% of Sales)	($1.40)
4	Gross Sales	$75.60
		Basis
5	**Cost of Goods Sold**	**$70.00**
6	Shrinkage	$70.00
7	Order Processing	$70.00
8	Credit Card Bank Fee @ 4%	4%
9	Premium Cost	$3.00
10	Returns Processing Cost Each	$5.00
11	Bad Debt	$75.60
12	Customer Service	$5.00
13	Shipping Expense	$3.00
14	Other Costs	$70.00
15	**Sub-Total Fulfillment Costs**	

Lines 6–14 detail fulfillment costs

Line 7 — Order Processing. Order processing might be calculated as a percent of sales (as is done in this model, at 5 percent of sales). Or, it might be a fixed amount.

Line 8 — Credit Card Bank Fee. Credit card fees will vary, but this model assumes 4 percent of gross sales. Importantly, this cost is only charged to the orders placed by customers who use credit cards. Illustration 4.3 illustrates that the 4 percent fee is charged to 80 percent of orders (Column D, Line 8), making the weighted average (Column E) as $2.42.

D	E	F
Percent of Sales	**Cost Per Sale**	**Percent Gross Sales**
40%	$28.00	37%
1%	$0.70	
5%	$3.50	
80%	$2.42	
100%	$3.00	
2%	$0.10	
0.5%	$0.38	
10%	$0.50	
100%	$3.00	
1%	$0.70	
	$14.30	19%

Line 9 – Premium Cost. If you give away anything free as an incentive for the customer to order, that cost is placed here and allocated to 100 percent of customers.

Line 10 — Returns Processing Cost Each. This represents the costs involved to accept returns, shipping (if you pay return shipping) and re-inventory.

Line 11 — Bad Debt. Any potential for bad debt, which could result from checks that do not clear or other chargebacks, should be accounted for in this line.

Line 12 — Customer Service. You might consider customer service to be part of overhead and choose to include it there. But if customer service is outsourced or can otherwise be separated from overhead, it can be included here. In this example, it is assumed the average customer service request costs $5.00 to process, and that 10 percent of customers (Column D) will require customer service assistance.

Line 13 — Shipping expense. This is your actual cost to ship the product.

Line 14 — Other costs. You may have other incidental costs, or costs you are uncertain of, that you can include in this line. In this example, it is assumed 1 percent of sales will have some type of other cost component.

Combined fulfillment costs are $14.30 in this example, or 19 percent of the gross sales dollar as shown in Illustration 4.3.

You may have other items that should be considered part of fulfillment or another cost that must be accounted for. You might place those in Line 14 or you may add new lines to your model. Here are a few additional items to consider:

- ▶ Customization or personalization cost
- ▶ Sales tax not collected
- ▶ BRE (Business Reply envelope) postage
- ▶ Shipping cost on exchanges
- ▶ Goods lost in shipment
- ▶ Cost of money – receivables

Overhead

Overhead is normally assigned a percent of sales. In Illustration 4.4, on pages 48–49, overhead is assumed to be 6 percent of sales, or $4.54 per first-time customer sale (E-16).

The model builds, on the next page, with the addition of overhead and marketing expenses.

Once you have identified your overhead number, you can arrive at how much of your sales dollar remains for marketing and profit. As illustrated in Illustration 4.4, the contribution to marketing and profit is $28.76 (E-17).

This Illustration goes a step further to identify an "allowable marketing cost" along with a required response rate. Your allowable marketing cost tells you how much you can spend to acquire a first-time customer.

Here's a line-by-line explanation of the remainder of this Illustration:

Line 18 — Pre-Tax Profit Objective. Simply stated, this is the percentage of sales you expect to make from a first-time customer. Yet, in some instances, you may choose to set the objective

Illustration 4.4

A	B	C
Line	**Item**	**Revenue**
1	Average First Time Product Sale	$70.00
2	Shipping Revenue (10% of Sales)	$7.00
3	Returns or Refunds (2% of Sales)	($1.40)
4	Gross Sales	$75.60
		Basis
5	**Cost of Goods Sold**	**$70.00**
6	Shrinkage	$70.00
7	Order Processing	$70.00
8	Credit Card Bank Fee @ 4%	4%
9	Premium Cost	$3.00
10	Returns Processing Cost Each	$5.00
11	Bad Debt	$75.60
12	Customer Service	$5.00
13	Shipping Expense	$3.00
14	Other Costs	$70.00
15	**Sub-Total Fulfillment Costs**	
16	**Overhead**	**$75.60**
17	Contribution to Marketing & Profit	
18	**Pre-Tax Profit Objective**	**$75.60**
19	**Allowable Marketing Cost per Customer**	
20	Promotion Cost per Thousand (/M)	$400.00
21	Required No. of Orders/M	
22	Required Response Percent	
23	**Total Percent of Dollar**	

at zero for first-time customers, assuming your profits come from established customers. But, in this example, 12 percent is assumed as the expected profit (D-18).

D	E	F
Percent of Sales	**Cost Per Sale**	**Percent Gross Sales**
40%	$28.00	37%
1%	$0.70	
5%	$3.50	
80%	$2.42	
100%	$3.00	
2%	$0.10	
0.5%	$0.38	
10%	$0.50	
100%	$3.00	
1%	$0.70	
	$14.30	19%
6%	$4.54	6%
	$28.76	
12%	$9.07	12%
	$19.69	26%
	20.3	
	2.03%	
		100%

Line 19 — Allowable Marketing Cost per Customer. This is what remains after all costs are deducted from the sales dollar. In this example, $19.69 is allowed to acquire a new customer (E-19). This is 26 percent of the sales dollar (F-19).

Line 20 — Promotion Cost per Thousand (/M). Taking these numbers a step further, you are able to determine what level of response you must achieve to make your numbers. This example assumes $400/M mailed for a direct mail package (based on rollout costs) (C-20).

Line 21 — Required Number of Orders per Thousand. This metric is calculated by dividing the promotion cost per thousand ($400) by the allowable marketing cost ($19.69). The required number of orders is 20.3 (E-21).

Line 22 — Required Response Percent. Dividing the required number of orders (20.3) by 1,000 mailed illustrates that the required response rate is 2.03 percent (E-22).

For comparison, had the profit objective been set at zero on Line 18, the allowable marketing cost would have been $28.76, with 13.9 orders per thousand required, or a response of 1.39 percent. Not requiring a profit on a first-time order sets the bar lower for required results.

Taken still another step, if overhead on Line 16 had been set at zero percent and the profit objective on Line 18 set at zero percent, the required response would have fallen from 2.03 percent to 1.20 percent, as shown in Illustration 4.5, on pages 52–53.

Use your spreadsheet for a range of "what if" scenarios.

Illustration 4.5

A	B	C
Line	**Item**	**Revenue**
1	Average First Time Product Sale	$70.00
2	Shipping Revenue (10% of Sales)	$7.00
3	Returns or Refunds (2% of Sales)	($1.40)
4	Gross Sales	$75.60
		Basis
5	**Cost of Goods Sold**	**$70.00**
6	Shrinkage	$70.00
7	Order Processing	$70.00
8	Credit Card Bank Fee @ 4%	4%
9	Premium Cost	$3.00
10	Returns Processing Cost Each	$5.00
11	Bad Debt	$75.60
12	Customer Service	$5.00
13	Shipping Expense	$3.00
14	Other Costs	$70.00
15	**Sub-Total Fulfillment Costs**	
16	**Overhead**	**$75.60**
17	Contribution to Marketing & Profit	
18	**Pre-Tax Profit Objective**	**$75.60**
19	**Allowable Marketing Cost per Customer**	
20	Promotion Cost per Thousand (/M)	$400.00
21	Required No. of Orders/M	
22	Required Response Percent	
23	**Total Percent of Dollar**	

D	E	F
Percent of Sales	**Cost Per Sale**	**Percent Gross Sales**
40%	**$28.00**	**37%**
1%	$0.70	
5%	$3.50	
80%	$2.42	
100%	$3.00	
2%	$0.10	
0.5%	$0.38	
10%	$0.50	
100%	$3.00	
1%	$0.70	
	$14.30	**19%**
0%	**$0.00**	**0%**
	$33.30	
0%	**$0.00**	**0%**
	$33.30	**44%**
	12.0	
	1.20%	
		100%

The Hennerberg Analytic Cycle

This flow chart represents the progression and relationships of the principals detailed in this book. The responsible Marketing Portfolio Manager never stops moving through the cycle, continually gathering more data, refining offers, initiating further testing, improving response rates.

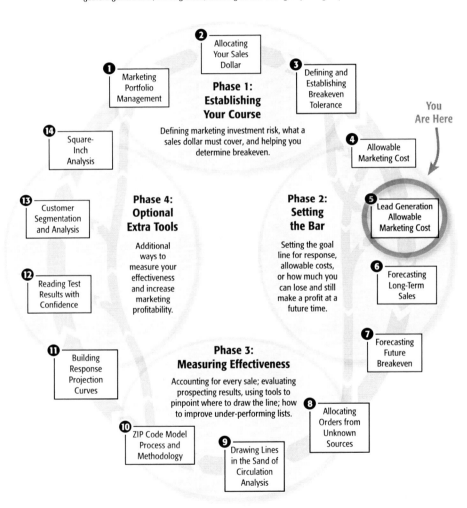

❷ Allocating Your Sales Dollar

❶ Marketing Portfolio Management

❸ Defining and Establishing Breakeven Tolerance

Phase 1: Establishing Your Course

Defining marketing investment risk, what a sales dollar must cover, and helping you determine breakeven.

You Are Here

❹ Allowable Marketing Cost

❶❹ Square-Inch Analysis

❶❸ Customer Segmentation and Analysis

Phase 4: Optional Extra Tools

Additional ways to measure your effectiveness and increase marketing profitability.

Phase 2: Setting the Bar

Setting the goal line for response, allowable costs, or how much you can lose and still make a profit at a future time.

❺ Lead Generation Allowable Marketing Cost

❶❷ Reading Test Results with Confidence

❻ Forecasting Long-Term Sales

❼ Forecasting Future Breakeven

❶❶ Building Response Projection Curves

Phase 3: Measuring Effectiveness

Accounting for every sale; evaluating prospecting results, using tools to pinpoint where to draw the line; how to improve under-performing lists.

❽ Allocating Orders from Unknown Sources

❶⓪ ZIP Code Model Process and Methodology

❾ Drawing Lines in the Sand of Circulation Analysis

Chapter 5

Lead Generation Allowable Marketing Cost

Lead generation programs are generally used when you need to pique the interest of a prospective buyer first and then sell her or him on your product or service over time. Often, the reason for taking more time to sell to your prospective customers is reflected in at least one of the following situations:

Read this chapter if you have a two-step sales program, are a business-to-business marketer, or generate leads for sales people.

A. You are selling an expensive product or service.

B. You have sales people making sales calls by phone or in person.

If your product or service has a higher than average price and likely can't be sold with a single contact, you probably will want to test the effect of a lead generation program. The first step of such a program utilizes a marketing approach that gets the interest of the prospective buyer, but doesn't close the sale just yet. When the prospective buyer expresses interest, you'll provide the prospect with more information or a follow-up call. Often, "more information" can be provided by mail in the form of a brochure, CD, or DVD. Delivery of streaming media can be done on a web site and may not seem costly, but the real expense lies in the production of the programming. Yet, while it's possible for delivery of the product demonstration to occur through the web, you still may find yourself sending a video, CD, or DVD along with the printed materials that a prospect can experience personally.

Considerations That Impact Marketing Numbers

For a lead generation program, there are a host of other considerations, all of which impact the marketing numbers, such as:

▶ **Cost of marketing** — As with any marketing program, you need to examine the cost of your initial inquiry mailing and fulfillment materials.

▶ **Cost to fulfill each inquiry** — You must develop a complete plan of action and materials to send to every inquiry. When you produce leads, you must do something with them. It won't do you any good to generate "tire kickers," so be mindful that unconverted leads cost you money.

Strengthening your conversion rate contributes significantly to bottom-line profit.

▶ **Conversion rate** — Whether the conversion comes from the expensive fulfillment package you have mailed or from a sales person, the percentage of conversions has a dramatic impact on your bottom-line profits.

▶ **Average purchase amount** — If you use a sales force to sell products or services that can result in frequent purchases, the average sale per customer has a dramatic impact on what you can spend on marketing. Future purchases measured over a long-time basis add significantly to your profitability.

▶ **Freebies or discounts** — Are you including a free premium item? Discounted price? Other costs to acquire the sale?

▶ **Sales call costs** — Sales calls are expensive and can cost hundreds of dollars per call. Qualifying the lead or reducing the number of calls to close

the sale is a powerful reason to use lead generation programs.

▶ **The second and all subsequent contacts** — What
happens when someone inquires about your
product and you mail a fulfillment package, but
generate no response? Does that inquiry fall into
a "black hole" never to be found again? Or do
you contact them over and over until it doesn't
make financial sense to pursue that lead?

Quantifying your cost to contact a cold prospect,
warm them up with a lead generation program, and
convert the prospect to a customer requires looking
at breakeven models differently than that of other
programs. One tool that can be used to quantify
the cost to acquire a customer is a Lead Generation
Allowable Cost model.

The model in Illustration 5.1, on pages 60–61,
assumes that you are using direct mail to generate
leads. The prospective customers generated are sent
product information via direct mail that is detailed
and therefore more expensive to produce than the
lead generation piece. Your web site may be a key
part of this program, and, if it is, your cost to fulfill
inquiries may not take the form of DVDs or expensive brochures. Nevertheless, even if the web is used
as the method of delivery, you will still have production costs associated with this program.

The spreadsheet shown in Illustration 5.1 provides
the same methodology as the Allowable Marketing Cost illustrations in Chapter 4. In this case,
the assumed average product sale is $1,200.00
(Column C, Line 1). Adding $60.00 for shipping
brings the total gross sale to $1,260.00 (C-3).

Cost of goods sold (COGS) is 35 percent (Column D, Line 4), or $420.00 (33 percent of gross sales). Fulfillment costs are detailed on Lines 5 through 11 of Column E and total $156.17 (12.4 percent of gross sales). Overhead is assumed at 8 percent of sales (D-13). Total COGS, fulfillment and overhead is $676.97 (E-14).

Inquiry fulfillment can be delivered by mail, web, or other means. In this case, the assumed cost to fulfill each inquiry is $10.00. Let us pause here and point out that to arrive at this assumed $10.00 cost, you must look at all costs associated with fulfilling an inquiry and arrive at an assumption of what it costs to fulfill each. It may only require adding the total annual cost of production, printed materials, broadcast-type materials (video or DVD), or costs of your web site associated with the cost to fulfill inquiries.

The cost to handle non-converting inquiries must be covered by sales to those who do convert.

If the cost to fulfill each inquiry is $10.00 and you historically convert 10 percent of your inquiries to a sale, then 90 percent of your inquiries did not convert. When that happens, you must allocate the cost to fulfill to those 90 percent of inquiries who did not convert to the 10 percent who did convert. To illustrate this in another way, if the fulfillment cost is $10.00 and there were 100 inquiries, the total inquiry fulfillment cost would be $1,000. If 10 percent of those 100 inquiries are converted to a sale (10 buyers), the remaining 90 inquiries that cost $10.00 each, or $900.00 total, must be absorbed by the 10 buyers who actually purchased. Or, $900.00 in inquiry fulfillment cost from non-buyers must be absorbed over 10 customers who did purchase, or $90.00 per buyer (E-18).

After deducting COGS, fulfillment, overhead, and inquiry fulfillment from gross sales, the contribution to marketing and profit is $483.03 (E-19). If the profit objective before taxes is 12 percent of gross sales ($151.20 from E-20), the allowable marketing cost per customer is $331.83 (E-21).

If the lead generation promotional cost is $500.00 per thousand (C-22), you must generate 1.5 converted orders per thousand (E-23) or 0.15 percent (E-24). But because of the nature of a two-step lead generation program, you must factor in the conversion rate which increases the gross response you need to make the numbers. In this example, we assume 10 percent of inquiries will convert to customers (D-16). This now means the inquiry response rate must be 1.51 percent (E-26).

Illustration 5.1

Line	Item	Revenue
1	Average Purchase	$1,200.00
2	Shipping Revenue (5% of Sales)	$60.00
3	Gross Sales	$1,260.00
		Basis
4	**Cost of Goods Sold**	**$1,200.00**
5	Order Processing	$10.00
6	Credit Card Bank Fee @ 4%	$1,260.00
7	Premium Cost	$25.00
8	Bad Debt	$1,260.00
9	Customer Service	$25.00
10	Shipping Expense	$50.00
11	Other Costs	$1,200.00
12	**Sub-Total Fulfillment Costs**	
13	**Overhead**	**$1,260.00**
14	**Total COGS, Fulfillment, Overhead**	
15	Inquiry Fulfillment Cost Each	$10.00
16	Inquiry Conversion Percentage	
17	Percentage Not Converted to Sale	
18	Total Inquiry Fulfillment Cost Absorbed per Customer	
19	Contribution to Marketing and Profit	
20	Profit Objective Before Taxes	$1,260.00
21	Allowable Marketing Cost per Customer	
22	Lead Generation Cost per Thousand (/M)	$500.00
23	Required Number of Converted Orders/M	
24	Required Conversion Response Percent	
25	Inquiry Conversion Percentage	
26	Required Gross Inquiry Response Percent	
27	**Total Percent of Dollar**	

Percent of Sales	Cost Per Conversion	Percent Gross Sales
35%	$420.00	33.3%
100%	$10.00	
80%	$40.32	
100%	$25.00	
1%	$12.60	
25%	$6.25	
100%	$50.00	
1%	$12.00	
	$156.17	12.4%
8%	$100.80	8.0%
	$676.97	
	$10.00	0.8%
10%		
90%		
	$90.00	7.1%
	$483.03	
12%	$151.20	12.0%
	$331.83	26.3%
	1.5	
	0.15%	
	10%	
	1.51%	
		100.0%

You must generate 1.51% response to make your numbers.

What-Ifs

It's always helpful to look at your own data with a few "what if" assumptions. Here is how the numbers change if we alter some of the assumptions in Illustration 5.1:

1. If we leave the inquiry fulfillment cost at $10, but we increase our conversion from 10 percent to 15 percent, the required gross response rate drops from 1.51 percent to 0.91 percent. That's a significant drop in required lead response if you can increase your closure rate.

2. If you increase your promotion cost from $500.00 per thousand to $600.00 per thousand, your required gross inquiry response rate climbs from 1.51 percent to 1.81 percent, or an increase of 20 percent. Production costs easily can go out of control, so if you had been spending $500.00 per thousand, but you decide to make creative changes and increase your cost, make sure you think through the overall impact of that $100.00 per thousand cost increase.

Leads for Sales People

In our next example, an Allowable Marketing Cost model is created for businesses that deploy sales people and use a lead generation program to generate and qualify leads to help the sales people be more productive.

Like in the prior example, it is important to determine what must be generated in response to make the program pay for itself. When you introduce the element of a sales force (as compared to selling your product directly to your end user), there are situations where you lose control of the numbers. Nevertheless, having benchmarks in place will help establish performance objectives.

Illustration 5.2, on pages 66–67, has many similarities to Illustration 5.1. But typically, when a sales person is used to sell the product, it is because the product is more involved and the average purchase will be substantially higher. It's also likely that conversion rates will be higher.

The primary differences between Illustrations 5.1 and 5.2 are:

▶ In this next example (Illustration 5.2), we will factor a customer's one-time purchase and long-term value. We will assume the definition of "long term" is one year, and the customer could purchase four times during the year.

▶ Sales call costs have been factored into the total marketing cost.

In lines 1 through 5, this model assumes there will be four purchase opportunities over the course of this one-year long-term purchase relationship. But it also

The cost of a personal sales call can be $500 or more. Use effective direct mail lead generation to make sales people more efficient.

assumes that not all customers will return to purchase a second time. In this example, it is assumed only 50 percent of the buyers return (C-2). Seventy-five percent of the 50 percent remaining purchase a third time (C-3), and 90 percent of those buying a third time will purchase a fourth time (C-4).

If we started with 100 customers, after one year there would be 34 remaining customers with cumulative purchases of 221, or an average of 2.21 purchases per customer.

Illustration 5.2 also has an additional column to compare one-time purchases to long-term purchases. Column E (lines 7 through 32) reports results from a single purchase, whereas Column F (lines 7 through 32) reveals long-term results.

Since sales people are involved, we assume the average purchase to be $5,000.00. Many of the same types of costs from Illustration 5.1 are noted in Illustration 5.2 on Lines 10 through 16, except those that do not apply in a traditional direct response situation. Like Illustration 5.1, inquiry fulfillment costs are calculated on Lines 18 through 21. Conversion is assumed to be 10 percent (D-19), meaning that each inquiry has to absorb $90.00 (E-21) in inquiry fulfillment costs.

Sales calls are estimated to cost $500.00 each (C-22), and it's assumed it takes three sales calls to close the first order; six during the course of the first-year relationship (D-23 and D-24). This leaves a contribution of $1,339.50 toward the first purchase (E-25), and $3,445.30 on a long-term value basis (F-25). After deducting the assumed 12 percent profit before tax objective, this leaves an allowable marketing cost of $739.50 for the first-time purchase (E-27), but justified to $2,119.30 if spread over a year's worth of purchases (F-27).

With a lead generation promotional cost of $500.00 per thousand (C-28), a gross inquiry response of 0.68 percent is required for the first purchase (E-32), or 0.24 percent (F-32) over the course of the year.

Illustration 5.2

A	B	C
Line	**Item**	**Retention Percent**
1	First Purchase	100%
2	Second Purchase	50%
3	Third Purchase	75%
4	Fourth Purchase	90%
5	Average Purchases/Customer	
6		**Revenue**
7	Average Purchase	$5,000.00
8	Net Sales Per Customer	
9		**Cost**
10	Cost Of Goods Sold (30% of Sales)	$1,500.00
11	Premium Cost	$25.00
12	Customer Service	$25.00
13	Overhead	
14	Delivery Expense	$100.00
15	**Sub-Total Costs**	
16	Cost Contingency	
17	**Total Costs**	
18	Inquiry Fulfillment Cost Each	$10.00
19	Inquiry Conversion Percentage	
20	Percentage Not Converted to Sale	
21	**Total Inquiry Fulfillment Cost Absorbed Per Customer**	
22	Sales Call Cost	$500.00
23	Number of Sales Calls Required to Close First Sale	
24	Number of Sales Calls Required Annually	
25	Contribution to Marketing and Profit	
26	Profit Before Tax Objective	
27	Allowable Marketing Cost Per Customer	
28	Promotion Cost Per Thousand	$500.00
29	Required Number of Converted Orders	
30	Required Conversion Response Percentage	
31	Sales Force Conversion Percentage	
32	Required Gross Inquiry Response	

D	E	F
	Number Of Customers	**Cumulative Purchases**
	100	100
	50	150
	38	188
	34	221
		2.21
	1st Purchase Revenue	**Long-Term Revenue**
	$5,000.00	$11,050.00
	$5,000.00	$11,050.00
Percent of Sales	**1st Purchase Cost**	**Long-Term Cost**
30%	$1,500.00	$3,315.00
100%	$25.00	$25.00
100%	$25.00	$25.00
8%	$400.00	$884.00
100%	$100.00	$221.00
	$2,050.00	**$4,470.00**
1%	$20.50	$44.70
	$2,070.50	**$4,514.70**
10%		
90%		
	$90.00	**$90.00**
3	$1,500.00	
6		$3,000.00
	$1,339.50	$3,445.30
12%	$600.00	$1,326.00
	$739.50	$2,119.30
	0.68	0.24
	0.068%	0.024%
	10%	10%
	0.68%	0.24%

The Hennerberg Analytic Cycle

This flow chart represents the progression and relationships of the principals detailed in this book. The responsible Marketing Portfolio Manager never stops moving through the cycle, continually gathering more data, refining offers, initiating further testing, improving response rates.

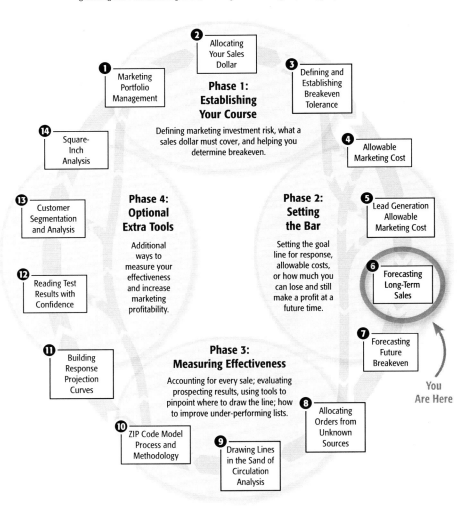

❶ Marketing Portfolio Management

❷ Allocating Your Sales Dollar

Phase 1: Establishing Your Course

Defining marketing investment risk, what a sales dollar must cover, and helping you determine breakeven.

❸ Defining and Establishing Breakeven Tolerance

❹ Allowable Marketing Cost

❺ Lead Generation Allowable Marketing Cost

❻ Forecasting Long-Term Sales

Phase 2: Setting the Bar

Setting the goal line for response, allowable costs, or how much you can lose and still make a profit at a future time.

❼ Forecasting Future Breakeven

You Are Here

❽ Allocating Orders from Unknown Sources

❾ Drawing Lines in the Sand of Circulation Analysis

Phase 3: Measuring Effectiveness

Accounting for every sale; evaluating prospecting results, using tools to pinpoint where to draw the line; how to improve under-performing lists.

❿ ZIP Code Model Process and Methodology

⓫ Building Response Projection Curves

⓬ Reading Test Results with Confidence

⓭ Customer Segmentation and Analysis

⓮ Square-Inch Analysis

Phase 4: Optional Extra Tools

Additional ways to measure your effectiveness and increase marketing profitability.

Chapter 6

Forecasting Long-Term Sales

Your foundation for evaluating the performance of your prospecting efforts is the Long-Term Sales model. The purpose of this model is to determine sales you can expect from a customer after "a long time."

Read this chapter if you lose money on your initial new customer acquisition.

If you bring on new customers at a loss, development of a Long-Term Sales model is essential. Once you have created this model, then you can take the next step of using this data to create a Forecasting Future Breakeven model, described in Chapter 7.

Developing your Long-Term Sales model will require having historical data, or at a minimum, sound assumptions that you are sure will be replicated in the marketplace. Specific data, or your best estimate, include the following:

1. Response rate percentage from first-time customers

2. Response rates from 2+ time customers

3. Average order value for each purchase

At this stage, acquisition marketing costs are not a factor in this model. In the next chapter, Forecasting Future Breakeven, we will quantify acceptable response threshold levels once we know what levels of retention we might expect based on the Long-Term Sales model.

Begin with 1,000 First-Time Customers

*Illustrations
6.1 – 6.5 continue
to build with
expanded data.*

Illustration 6.1 sets the stage for where to begin. The example begins with 1,000 new customers acquired during a prospecting effort. Whether these customers were acquired by mail, e-mail marketing, print, or any other medium does not impact how the model is set up. However, the media used to acquire new customers is relevant when looking at subsequent purchases. Generally, a customer acquired via a direct mail solicitation will have a better repeat purchase rate than customers acquired in other media, but to set your own standards, you should closely track your own new customer performance by medium.

Illustration 6.1

A	B	C
Line	Item	Original Acquisition
1	Original Acquisition	1,000
2	% Retention	100.0%
3	Purchases (Orders)	1,000
4	Average Order	$70
5	Sales	$70,000
6	Purchases per Contact Cycle	1,000
7	Cumulative Customer Purchases	1,000
8	Average Purchases/Customer Acquired	1.00
9	Total Sales	$70,000
10	Cumulative Sales	$70,000
11	Average Long-Term Sales Value	$70.00

In Illustration 6.1, we begin with 1,000 customers (C-1) in the original acquisition. The average order is assumed to be $70.00 (C-4), generating $70,000 in sales (C-5). Since we have only sold them this first time, the purchase per contact cycle is 1.00 (C-8).

Total sales (C-9) and cumulative sales (C-10) are $70,000. Importantly, if we were to stop marketing to these 1,000 customers now, the value of the customer would remain at $70.00 (C-11).

Second-Time Buyers

The Illustration expands with future marketing to those 1,000 customers. You should contact a first-time buyer as quickly as you can to optimize the impact of your first sale and to get the customer in a pattern of buying from you again. As it is often said in direct marketing, the most important sale isn't your first one; it's the second sale. Your track record of converting first-time buyers into second-time buyers is essential to development of this model. If you don't have this data available, you should make it a high priority to implement ways to track sales from first-time buyers through the assignment of a unique key or source codes to first-time buyers in future marketing efforts. If you don't have actual data, you'll have to make assumptions.

Illustration 6.2, on page 72, is expanded from Illustration 6.1 to include the first contact with first-time buyers. The following assumptions are made:

Illustration 6.2 is the same as 6.1, with the addition of Column D.

1. Response of 10 percent (D-2) from first-time buyers. Response rates often are significantly higher from a new buyer than what is generated from a prospect. This yields 100 orders (D-3).

2. Higher average order of $84.00 (D-4), as compared to $70.00 in the original acquisition. In this case, it is assumed the repeat average order will be 20 percent higher than the average order in the original acquisition.

Illustration 6.2

A	B	C	D
Line	Item	Original Acquisition	1st Contact With First-Time Buyers
1	Original Acquisition	1,000	1,000
2	% Retention	100.0%	10.0%
3	Purchases (Orders)	1,000	100
4	Average Order	$70	$84
5	Sales	$70,000	$8,400
6	Purchases per Contact Cycle	1,000	100
7	Cumulative Customer Purchases	1,000	1,100
8	Average Purchases/Customer Acquired	1.00	1.10
9	Total Sales	$70,000	$8,400
10	Cumulative Sales	$70,000	$78,400
11	Average Long-Term Sales Value	$70.00	$78.40

The addition of this next contact now reveals improvement in the Long-Term Sales Value. Now, the initial 1,000 one-time customers (C-1) have turned into 1,100 purchases (D-7), or a ratio of 1.10 purchases per customer (D-8). Cumulative sales are now $78,400 ($70,000 from the original customer acquisition effort plus $8,400 from the first contact with these newly acquired customers) (D-10). Average Long-Term Sales Value now increases to $78.40 (D-11).

Second Customer Contact

When we extend these assumptions to the second contact, our Long-Term Sales Value continues to increase. In this second contact, you have the opportunity to learn more about customer response behavior and how it impacts your overall profitability.

Examining Illustration 6.3 on pages 74–75, your original 1,000 customers now can be divided into two groups: Two-Time Buyers (Column E) and Non-Active Buyers (Column F). The 100 Two-Time Buyers (E-1) are responders from the first contact. The 900 Non-Active Buyers (F-1) didn't respond to the first contact, but some will respond to your second contact. In all likelihood, the Non-Active Buyers won't respond as well as the Two-Time Buyers, so these assumptions are made:

1. Two-Time Buyers who purchased from both the acquisition and first contact should respond well. This model assumes 15 percent will purchase a third time (E-2). They have an average order of $84.00 (E-4).

2. Non-Active Buyers are assumed to respond at a 5 percent rate (F-2). An $84.00 average order (F-4), 20 percent higher than the original average order, is assumed because this will be their second purchase.

3. In this second contact cycle, we yield 15 purchases (E-3) from Two-Time Buyers and 45 (F-3) from Non-Active Buyers. Cumulative Purchases are now up to 1,160 (F-7).

4. Average purchases per customer from the original 1,000 customers raises to 1.16 (F-8).

5. The $5,040 in sales (F-9) from this second contact brings Cumulative Sales to $83,440 (F-10). Your average customer's Long-Term Sales Value has now risen to $83.44 (F-11).

The second time you contact new customers, you should segment them as follows: (1) those who responded to the first contact after they were acquired, and (2) those who did not respond to the first contact after they were acquired.

Illustration 6.3

A	B
Line	Item
1	Original Acquisition
2	% Retention
3	Purchases (Orders)
4	Average Order
5	Sales
6	Purchases per Contact Cycle
7	Cumulative Customer Purchases
8	Average Purchases/Customer Acquired
9	Total Sales
10	Cumulative Sales
11	Average Long-Term Sales Value

Future Customer Contact

The assumptions continue step-by-step, contact-by-contact on Illustrations 6.4 and 6.5. The two segments of customers are continued: 2+ Time Buyers and Non-Active Buyers. An option would be to track 3+ customers, 4+ customers, etc., as separate segments within your customer database.

In Illustrations 6.4 and 6.5, on pages 76–77, response from 2+ Time Buyers remains at 15 percent (Line 2, Columns G, I, K, M). But response from Non-Active Buyers gradually declines over time, with the assumption that, with each passing contact cycle, non-buyers who didn't buy a second time in an earlier mailing are less and less likely to buy again. Response drops to 4 percent on the third contact (H-2), 3 percent in the fourth contact (J-2), 2 percent in the fifth contact (L-2), and 1 percent in the sixth contact (N-2). At some point it no longer makes

C	D	E	F
Original Acquisition	**1st Contact With First-Time Buyers**	**2nd Contact With 2-Time Buyers**	**2nd Contact With Non-Active Buyers**
1,000	1,000	100	900
100.0%	10.0%	15.0%	5.0%
1,000	100	15	45
$70	$84	$84	$84
$70,000	$8,400	$1,260	$3.780
1,000	100	15.00	45.00
1,000	1,100		1,160
1.00	1.10		1.16
$70,000	$8,400		$5,040
$70,000	$78,400		$83,440
$70.00	$78.40		$83.44

financial sense to contact Non-Active Buyers, who have never responded to a subsequent offer. However, if as a group they still purchase at a higher rate than that of prospects, you may choose to mail them as prospects. Keep in mind that when you acquire a customer, you do not have to pay list rental expense to mail this name in future mailings, which reduces your marketing cost.

Average purchases are now 1,160 from the original 1,000 acquired. This combines 1,000 original purchases, 100 first contact purchases, and 60 second contact purchases.

The bottom line average Long-Term Sales Value increases with each contact. On the third contact, the Long-Term Sales Value increases to $88.14 per customer (H-11). After the fourth contact, the Long-Term Sales Value increases to $92.51 (J-11). After the fifth contact, it increases to $96.46 (L-11). And, after the sixth contact, where this model ends, the average Long-Term Sales Value is $99.90 (N-11). Of course, you have the option of carrying out the model farther.

Illustration 6.4

A	B
Line	**Item**
1	Original Acquisition
2	% Retention
3	Purchases (Orders)
4	Average Order
5	Sales
6	Purchases per Contact Cycle
7	Cumulative Customer Purchases
8	Average Purchases/Customer Acquired
9	Total Sales
10	Cumulative Sales
11	Average Long-Term Sales Value

Illustration 6.5

A	B
Line	**Item**
1	Original Acquisition
2	% Retention
3	Purchases (Orders)
4	Average Order
5	Sales
6	Purchases per Contact Cycle
7	Cumulative Customer Purchases
8	Average Purchases/Customer Acquired
9	Total Sales
10	Cumulative Sales
11	Average Long-Term Sales Value

With the identified Long-Term Sales Value, we now
can build upon this key data point and create a Future
Breakeven model (described in the next chapter)

G	H	I	J
3rd Contact With 2+ -Time Buyers	3rd Contact With Non-Active Buyers	4th Contact With 2+ -Time Buyers	4th Contact With Non-Active Buyers
145	855	179	821
15%	4%	15%	3%
22	34	27	25
$84	$84	$84	$84
$1,848	$2,856	$2,268	$2,100
22	34	27	25
	1,216		1,268
	1.22		1.27
	$4,704		$4,368
	$88,144		$92,512
	$88.14		$92.51

K	L	M	N
5th Contact With 2+ -Time Buyers	5th Contact With Non-Active Buyers	6th Contact With 2+ -Time Buyers	6th Contact With Non-Active Buyers
204	796	220	780
15%	2%	15%	1%
31	16	33	8
$84	$84	$84	$84
$2,604	$1,344	$2,772	$672
31	16	33	8
	1,315		1,356
	1.32		1.36
	$3,948		$3,444
	$96,460		$99,904
	$96.46		$99.90

that considers the Long-Term Sales Value, cost of goods sold (COGS), fulfillment, overhead, marketing expense, and contribution to profit.

Investments In Future Contacts

Each successful contact with new customers in a group will increase the overall average value of customers within the group. If 1,000 first-time customers are acquired with an average sale of $70.00, after another six contacts, the sales from customers who respond to future marketing has the potential to grow to an average of $99.90 for the 1,000 customers initially acquired, as demonstrated in this chapter.

Illustration 6.6

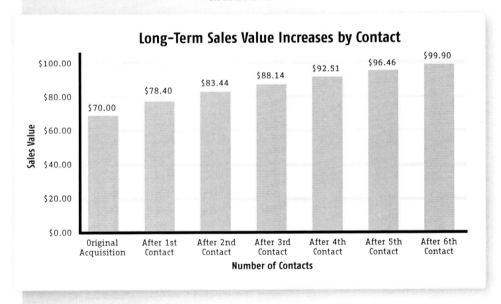

Long-Term Sales Value Increases by Contact

The Hennerberg Analytic Cycle

This flow chart represents the progression and relationships of the principals detailed in this book. The responsible Marketing Portfolio Manager never stops moving through the cycle, continually gathering more data, refining offers, initiating further testing, improving response rates.

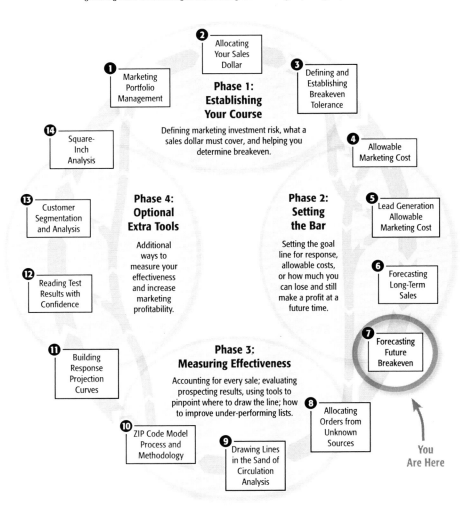

2 Allocating Your Sales Dollar

1 Marketing Portfolio Management

3 Defining and Establishing Breakeven Tolerance

Phase 1: Establishing Your Course

Defining marketing investment risk, what a sales dollar must cover, and helping you determine breakeven.

14 Square-Inch Analysis

4 Allowable Marketing Cost

13 Customer Segmentation and Analysis

Phase 4: Optional Extra Tools

Additional ways to measure your effectiveness and increase marketing profitability.

Phase 2: Setting the Bar

Setting the goal line for response, allowable costs, or how much you can lose and still make a profit at a future time.

5 Lead Generation Allowable Marketing Cost

12 Reading Test Results with Confidence

6 Forecasting Long-Term Sales

7 Forecasting Future Breakeven

11 Building Response Projection Curves

Phase 3: Measuring Effectiveness

Accounting for every sale; evaluating prospecting results, using tools to pinpoint where to draw the line; how to improve under-performing lists.

8 Allocating Orders from Unknown Sources

10 ZIP Code Model Process and Methodology

9 Drawing Lines in the Sand of Circulation Analysis

You Are Here

Chapter 7

Forecasting Future Breakeven

Now that you have a Long-Term Sales Value Model, you can determine at what future point you will breakeven. In Chapter 3, we defined four possible breakeven scenarios:

1. The minimum sales dollars needed to recover marketing, cost of goods sold (COGS), fulfillment, overhead, plus a targeted profit.

2. The minimum sales dollars needed to recover marketing, COGS, fulfillment, plus overhead. Profit is not required.

3. The minimum sales dollars needed to recover marketing, COGS, and fulfillment. Overhead would not be covered and profit is not required.

4. The minimum sales dollar loss you can tolerate on the first order to breakeven at a future date.

Breakeven scenario No. 4 provides the greatest flexibility to acquire new customers.

To build upon the Long-Term Sales Value model, you'll need to know your COGS, fulfillment, overhead, and marketing expenses.

For COGS, fulfillment and overhead, it likely will be easier to use a percentage of sales. If you don't know that number, your finance department should be able to give you reliable percentages. For marketing expenses, you should use a fixed dollar amount expressed in cost per thousand.

Illustration 7.1, on pages 82–83, further defines several terms used in the Long-Term Sales Value model.

Illustration 7.1

Line	Term
1	Mail Quantity
2	Response Rate
3	No. Resp.
4	Average Order
5	S&H Percent of Avg Order
6	Avg Order Including S&H
7	Marketing CPM
8	Marketing Cost
9	Mail Quantity
10	Purchases (Orders)
11	Total Sales Dollars
12	Sales / M
13	Cumulative Sales
14	Total Marketing Cost
15	Marketing Cost Per Order
16	Cumulative Marketing Cost
17	Average Long-Term Sales Value
18	Average Purchase Frequency
19	Gross Margin
20	COGS
21	Fulfillment
22	Overhead Allocation
23	Profit Contribution
24	Profit Per Thousand
25	Carryover Profit (Loss)
26	Cumulative Contribution
27	Contribution Percent of Cumulative Sales
28	ROI on Marketing Investment

C
Definition
Mail volume, or circulation, from original acquisition
Actual percentage response
Actual number of customers (or starters) acquired
Average dollar amount spent by each customer
If you charge shipping & handling, and the amount of S&H varies, express it as a percentage of your average order
Combined average order and S&H
Your cost of marketing expressed on a cost per thousand basis
Marketing cost per thousand multiplied by actual mail quantity or circulation
Total number of pieces mailed
Total purchases or orders
Total sales dollars from this effort
Sales per one thousand mailed
The accumulation of sales from the current effort and all previous efforts
Cost to mail all customer segments
Cost of marketing divided by orders
The accumulation of marketing costs from the current effort and all previous efforts
Total sales divided by the original starter number. In this model, the original starter number is 1,000 customers
Average times a customer has purchased. The formula takes the Cumulative Sales divided by the original number of starters.
Sales minus marketing cost from this contact
Actual cost of goods, usually expressed as a percentage of sales
See Chapter 2 for a list of items typically included in fulfillment
Usually expressed as a percent of sales
Gross margin minus COGS minus fulfillment, and minus overhead allocation
Profit contribution divided by circulation in thousands
The amount of profit or loss carried over from the previous contact
Ongoing cumulative profit contribution (or loss) from line 25
Percent of line 26
Percent of gain from the marketing investment dollars spent.

Using the line-by-line definitions in Illustration 7.1 as a basis for understanding Illustration 7.2, you'll see that several assumptions have been made. Key among them are items in Column C, Lines 20, 21 and 22. This model assumes COGS is 37 percent of sales and shipping and handling (S&H); fulfillment is 19 percent of sales and S&H; and overhead is zero. You have the option of calculating COGS based on sales only (excluding S&H) if you choose. Including S&H in this model assumes a more conservative calculation. A note about fulfillment: The income of S&H is accounted for on Lines 5 and 6, but the expense of shipping is accounted for as a cost in Line 21.

The bottom line with this portion of the model is that in the original acquisition you will lose money, even with no allocation of expenses to overhead. As shown in Illustration 7.2, the loss per thousand mailed in this original acquisition is $174.00 (D-24).

This model continues through Illustration 7.8.

With this loss of $22,831 (D-23), it's clear the second order and future orders from this group of 1,000 newly acquired customers are critical to profitability.

Illustration 7.2

A	B	C	D
Line	**Item**	**%**	**Original Acquisition**
1	Mail Quantity		131,579
2	Resp. Rate		0.76%
3	No. Resp.		1,000
4	Average Order		$70.00
5	S&H Percent of Avg Order		10%
6	Avg Order Including S&H		$77.00
7	Mktg CPM		$431.00
8	Mktg Cost		$56,711
9	Mail Quantity		131,579
10	Purchases (Orders)		1,000
11	Total Sales		$77,000
12	Sales / M		$585
13	Cumulative Sales		$77,000
14	Total Mktg Cost		$56,711
15	Marketing Cost Per Order		$56.71
16	Cumulative Marketing Cost		$56,711
17	Average Long-Term Sales Value		$77.00
18	Average Purchase Frequency		1.00
19	Gross Margin		$20,289
20	COGS	37%	$28,490
21	Fulfillment	19%	$14,630
22	Overhead Allocation	0%	–
23	Profit Contribution		$(22,831)
24	Profit Per Thousand (Original Acq)		$(174)
25	Carryover Profit (Loss)		$(22,831)
26	Cumulative Contribution		$(22,831)
27	Contribution Percent of Cumulative Sales		-29.7%
28	ROI on Marketing Investment		-40.3%

It costs $56.71 to acquire a new customer in this model.

In Illustration 7.3, we expand the model to include results from the second contact with these 1,000 first-time buyers. We assume that the second contact produces a response rate of 10 percent (E-2), with the average order increasing to $84.00 (E-4), reflecting a 20 percent increase over the original acquisition. The average order, including S&H, is now $92.40 (E-6). We further assume that the marketing cost per thousand has dropped to $350.00 (E-7) from $431.00 in the original acquisition (D-7). This assumes list rental cost was $81.00 in the original acquisition, which is no longer a cost for marketing to these buyers. While this second effort on its own shows a profit contribution of $3,715 (E-23), when the carryover loss of $22,831 is included (E-25), we still show a loss of $19,116 (E-26).

List rental cost disappears as a marketing cost, once you acquire a customer.

Illustration 7.3

A	B	C	D	E
Line	Item	%	Original Acquisition	1st Contact With First-Time Buyer
1	Mail Quantity		131,579	1,000
2	Response Rate		0.76%	10.0%
3	No. of Responses		1,000	100
4	Average Order		$70	$84
5	S&H Percent of Average Order		10%	10%
6	Avg Order Including S&H		$77.00	$92.40
7	Mktg CPM		$431	$350
8	Mktg Cost		$56,711	$350
9	Mail Quantity		131,579	1,000
10	Purchases (Orders)		1,000	100
11	Total Sales		$77,000	$9,240
12	Sales / M		$585	$9,240
13	Cumulative Sales		$77,000	$86,240
14	Total Marketing Cost		$56,711	$350
15	Marketing Cost Per Order		$56.71	$3.50
16	Cumulative Marketing Cost		$56,711	$57,061
17	Average Long-Term Sales Value		$77.00	$86.24
18	Average Purchase Frequency		1.00	1.10
19	Gross Margin		$20,289	$8,890
20	COGS	37%	$28,490	$3,419
21	Fulfillment	19%	$14,630	$1,756
22	Overhead Allocation	0%	–	–
23	Profit Contribution		$(22,831)	$3,715
24	Profit Per Thousand (Original Acq.)		$(174)	
25	Carryover Profit (Loss)		$(22,831)	$(22,831)
26	Cumulative Contribution		$(22,831)	$(19,116)
27	Contribution % of Cumulative Sales		-29.7%	-22.2%
28	ROI on Marketing Investment		-40.3%	-33.5%

By the second contact (Illustration 7.4) with this
original group of 1,000 customers, we make progress
toward recovering lost money, but have a distance
to go before breaking even on these new customers.

Illustration 7.4

A	B	C
Line	**Item**	**%**
1	Mail Quantity	
2	Resp. Rate	
3	No. Resp.	
4	Average Order	
5	S&H Percent of Average Order	
6	Avg Order Including S&H	
7	Mktg CPM	
8	Mktg Cost	
9	Mail Quantity	
10	Purchases (Orders)	
11	Total Sales	
12	Sales / M	
13	Cumulative Sales	
14	Total Mktg Cost	
15	Marketing Cost Per Order	
16	Cumulative Marketing Cost	
17	Avg. Long-Term Sales Value	
18	Average Purchase Frequency	
19	Gross Margin	
20	COGS	37%
21	Fulfillment	19%
22	Overhead Allocation	0%
23	Profit Contribution	
24	Profit/M (Original Acq)	
25	Carryover Profit (Loss)	
26	Cumulative Contribution	
27	Contribution Percent of Cumulative Sales	
28	ROI on Marketing Investment	

This expanded portion of the model now illustrates that, after the second contact, we have a cumulative loss of $17,026 (G-26).

D	E	F	G
Original Acquisition	**1st Contact With First-Time Buyer**	**2nd Contact With 2-Time Buyers**	**2nd Contact With Non-Active Buyers**
131,579	1,000	100	900
0.76%	10.0%	15.0%	5.0%
1,000	100	15	45
$70	$84	$84	$84
10%	10%	10%	10%
$77.00	$92.40	$92.40	$92.40
$431	$350	$350	$350
$56,711	$350	$35	$315
131,579	1,000		1,000
1,000	100		60
$77,000	$9,240		$5,544
$585	$9,240		$5,544
$77,000	$86,240		$91,784
$56,711	$350		$350
$56.71	$3.50		$5.83
$56,711	$57,061		$57,411
$77.00	$86.24		$91.78
1.00	1.10		1.16
$20,289	$8,890		$5,194
$28,490	$3,419		$2,051
$14,630	$1,756		$1,053
–	–		–
$(22,831)	$3,715		$2,090
$(174)			
$(22,831)	$(22,831)		$(19,116)
$(22,831)	$(19,116)		$(17,026)
-29.7%	-22.2%		-18.6%
-40.3%	-33.5%		-29.7%

The results from the 1,000 starter customers in Columns F and G are combined in Column G, Lines 9–28

Illustrations 7.5, 7.6, 7.7, and 7.8 complete the
model, to reveal that we will breakeven from this
group of 1,000 customers in the ninth contact cycle.

Illustration 7.5

A	B	C
Line	**Item**	**%**
1	Mail Quantity	
2	Resp. Rate	
3	No. Resp.	
4	Average Order	
5	S&H Percent of Average Order	
6	Avg Order Including S&H	
7	Mktg CPM	
8	Mktg Cost	
9	Mail Quantity	
10	Purchases (Orders)	
11	Total Sales	
12	Sales / M	
13	Cumulative Sales	
14	Total Mktg Cost	
15	Marketing Cost Per Order	
16	Cumulative Marketing Cost	
17	Average Long-Term Sales Value	
18	Average Purchase Frequency	
19	Gross Margin	
20	COGS	37%
21	Fulfillment	19%
22	Overhead Allocation	0%
23	Profit Contribution	
24	Profit/M (Original Acq)	
25	Carryover Profit (Loss)	
26	Cumulative Contribution	
27	Contribution Percent of Cumulative Sales	
28	ROI on Marketing Investment	

H	I	J	K
3rd Contact With 2+ Time Buyers	3rd Contact With Non-Active Buyers	4th Contact With 2+ Time Buyers	4th Contact With Non-Active Buyers
145	855	188	812
15.0%	5.0%	15.0%	5.0%
22	43	28	41
$84	$84	$84	$84
10%	10%	10%	10%
$92.40	$92.40	$92.40	$92.40
$350	$350	$350	$350
$51	$299	$66	$284
	1,000		1,000
	65		69
	$6,006		$6,376
	$6,006		$6,376
	$97,790		$104,166
	$350		$350
	$5.38		$5.07
	$57,761		$58,111
	$97.79		$104.17
	1.22		1.29
	$5,656		$6,026
	$2,222		$2,359
	$1,141		$1,211
	$2,293		$2,456
	$(17,026)		$(14,733)
	$(14,733)		$(12,277)
	-15.1%		-11.8%
	-25.5%		-21.1%

Illustration 7.6

Line	Item	%
1	Mail Quantity	
2	Resp. Rate	
3	No. Resp.	
4	Average Order	
5	S&H Percent of Average Order	
6	Avg Order Including S&H	
7	Mktg CPM	
8	Mktg Cost	
9	Mail Quantity	
10	Purchases (Orders)	
11	Total Sales	
12	Sales / M	
13	Cumulative Sales	
14	Total Mktg Cost	
15	Marketing Cost Per Order	
16	Cumulative Marketing Cost	
17	Average Long-Term Sales Value	
18	Average Purchase Frequency	
19	Gross Margin	
20	COGS	37%
21	Fulfillment	19%
22	Overhead Allocation	0%
23	Profit Contribution	
24	Profit/M (Original Acq)	
25	Carryover Profit (Loss)	
26	Cumulative Contribution	
27	Contribution Percent of Cumulative Sales	
28	ROI on Marketing Investment	

L	M	N	O
5th Contact With 2+ Time Buyers	**5th Contact With Non-Active Buyers**	**6th Contact With 2+ Time Buyers**	**6th Contact With Non-Active Buyers**
229	771	268	732
15.0%	5.0%	15.0%	4.0%
34	39	40	29
$84	$84	$84	$84
10%	10%	10%	10%
$92.40	$92.40	$92.40	$92.40
$350	$350	$350	$350
$80	$270	$94	$256
	1,000		1,000
	73		69
	$6,745		$6,376
	$6,745		$6,376
	$110,911		$117,287
	$350		$350
	$4.79		$5.07
	$58,461		$58,811
	$110.91		$117.29
	1.37		1.44
	$6,395		$6,026
	$2,496		$2,359
	$1,282		$1,211
	$2,617		$2,456
	$(12,277)		$(9,660)
	$(9,660)		$(7,204)
	-8.7%		-6.1%
	-16.5%		-12.2%

Illustration 7.7

A	B	C
Line	Item	%
1	Mail Quantity	
2	Resp. Rate	
3	No. Resp.	
4	Average Order	
5	S&H Percent of Average Order	
6	Avg Order Including S&H	
7	Mktg CPM	
8	Mktg Cost	
9	Mail Quantity	
10	Purchases (Orders)	
11	Total Sales	
12	Sales / M	
13	Cumulative Sales	
14	Total Mktg Cost	
15	Marketing Cost Per Order	
16	Cumulative Marketing Cost	
17	Average Long-Term Sales Value	
18	Average Purchase Frequency	
19	Gross Margin	
20	COGS	37%
21	Fulfillment	19%
22	Overhead Allocation	0%
23	Profit Contribution	
24	Profit/M (Original Acq)	
25	Carryover Profit (Loss)	
26	Cumulative Contribution	
27	Contribution Percent of Cumulative Sales	
28	ROI on Marketing Investment	

P	Q	R	S
7th Contact With 2+ Time Buyers	7th Contact With Non-Active Buyers	8th Contact With 2+ Time Buyers	8th Contact With Non-Active Buyers
297	703	322	678
15.0%	3.5%	15.0%	3.0%
45	25	48	20
$84	$84	$84	$84
10%	10%	10%	10%
$92.40	$92.40	$92.40	$92.40
$350	$350	$350	$350
$104	$246	$113	$237
	1,000		1,000
	70		68
	$6,468		$6,283
	$6,468		$6,283
	$123,755		$130,038
	$350		$350
	$5.00		$5.15
	$59,161		$59,511
	$123.75		$130.04
	1.51		1.57
	$6,118		$5,933
	$2,393		$2,325
	$1,229		$1,194
	$2,496		$2,414
	$(7,204)		$(4,708)
	$(4,708)		$(2,294)
	-3.8%		-1.8%
	-8.0%		-3.9%

Illustration 7.8

A	B	C	T	U
Line	Item	%	9th Contact With 2+ Time Buyers	9th Contact With Non-Active Buyers
1	Mail Quantity		342	658
2	Resp. Rate		15.0%	2.5%
3	No. Resp.		51	16
4	Average Order		$84	$84
5	S&H Percent of Average Order		10%	10%
6	Avg Order Including S&H		$92.40	$92.40
7	Mktg CPM		$350	$350
8	Mktg Cost		$120	$230
9	Mail Quantity			1,000
10	Purchases (Orders)			67
11	Total Sales			$6,191
12	Sales / M			$6,191
13	Cumulative Sales			$136,229
14	Total Mktg Cost			$350
15	Marketing Cost Per Order			$5.22
16	Cumulative Marketing Cost			$59,861
17	Average Long-Term Sales Value			$136.23
18	Average Purchase Frequency			1.64
19	Gross Margin			$5,841
20	COGS	37%		$2,291
21	Fulfillment	19%		$1,176
22	Overhead Allocation	0%		
23	Profit Contribution			$2,374
24	Profit/M (Original Acq)			
25	Carryover Profit (Loss)			$(2,294)
26	Cumulative Contribution			$80
27	Contribution Percent of Cumulative Sales			0.1%
28	ROI on Marketing Investment			0.1%

The marketing ROI finally reaches a positive percentage and breaks even after the ninth contact.

Breakeven is now achieved in the ninth contact when the ROI on Marketing Investment (U-28) finally reaches a positive percentage. It should be noted that this model does not consider financial accounting principles, such as the cost of money using a net present value calculation. You should work with your finance staff to factor in the cost of money, which will extend breakeven out somewhat farther.

Breakeven When Overhead is Recovered

If your breakeven requirement is to recover 6 percent overhead (if zero percent were to become 6 percent in Line 22) in addition to recovering COGS, fulfillment, overhead, and marketing costs, it could require 13 or more contacts to breakeven.

If you have to recover overhead, the breakeven stretches from 9 to 13 or more contacts.

The Hennerberg Analytic Cycle

This flow chart represents the progression and relationships of the principals detailed in this book. The responsible Marketing Portfolio Manager never stops moving through the cycle, continually gathering more data, refining offers, initiating further testing, improving response rates.

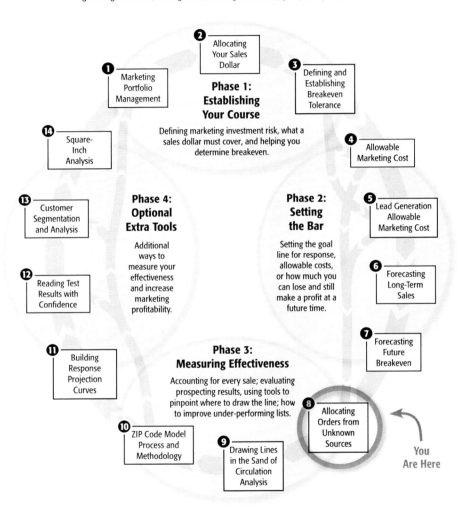

Chapter 8

Allocating Orders From Unknown Sources

Almost every direct marketing business receives orders from unknown sources that cannot be related to a key code or source code. Even the best of marketers, who carefully assign key codes to every effort and train order entry staff to ask callers for codes, will have orders from miscellaneous unknown sources. Orders placed on web sites often are difficult to track back to an offline medium. Did the customer place the order online because of something received in the mail? Did he or she see an ad online or in print? Did he or she find you via organic or paid search?

There often are dozens of "miscellaneous" descriptions that attempt to categorize the sources of these untraceable orders: "brochure," "friend," "insert," "ordered last year," "received as gift," and more.

At the end of a campaign or season, it is important that you examine your volume of orders from a broad-based perspective and understand what percentage of orders you receive from unknown sources. Some marketers may choose to simply view those orders and sales as icing on the cake that feels like found money. But taking that view shortchanges the results of your other marketing activity. If you don't match back unknown orders to known order sources, you miss knowing the complete picture.

If you choose not to allocate miscellaneous orders and sales, you shortchange your overall results.

Consider the scenario from Illustration 8.1, on pages 100–101. In this example, Miscellaneous/Unknown orders were 34,293 (Column D, Line 6), or 11.3

Illustration 8.1

A	B	C	D	E
Line	Item	Circulation	Orders	% Response
1	Customers	2,438,793	182,909	7.50%
2	Prospecting	5,093,992	34,639	0.68%
3	Inserts	10,000,000	2,532	0.03%
4	Space Ads	7,000,000	7,147	0.10%
5	Web Orders		42,948	
6	Misc./Unknown		34,293	
7	**Total All Sources**		**304,468**	

percent of total orders (H-6) and 9.3 percent of total sales (I-6).

One approach to account for this activity is to allocate back to each list or medium a proportion of orders and sales from "unknown" and "miscellaneous" sources. If, for example, 80 percent of your business comes from customers and 20 percent of your business comes from prospecting, you should allocate 80 percent of "unknown/miscellaneous" orders to customers. On an individual customer segment key code or prospecting list, you should calculate its percentage of the total orders and reallocate that same percentage of "unknown/miscellaneous" orders to that segment.

Expanding upon the numbers from Illustration 8.1, we show in Illustrations 8.2, 8.3, and 8.4, on pages 102–105, what happens when you allocate miscellaneous orders across quantifiable sources.

Illustrations 8.2, 8.3, and 8.4 (which actually are portions of one horizontally long spreadsheet comprising Columns A-Q) use the same categories and number of orders, but take the first step toward enabling us to reallocate orders. Line 8, Orders Excluding

F	G	H	I
Average Order	**Sales**	**Orders % of Total**	**Sales % of Total**
$87.42	$15,989,946	60.1%	67.7%
$64.82	$2,245,284	11.4%	9.5%
$54.46	$137,884	0.8%	0.6%
$56.29	$402,305	2.3%	1.7%
$61.49	$2,640,873	14.1%	11.2%
$63.93	$2,192,351	11.3%	9.3%
$77.54	**$23,608,643**	**100.0%**	**100.0%**

Misc./Unk., has been added to provide the basis for reallocation. Doing this, we will allocate orders and sales on a weighted average basis across customers, prospecting, inserts, space ads and web orders. The premise is that orders can be initiated by any media, but not all orders are necessarily tracked correctly. For example, customers may read a key code wrong when phoning in an order. People who found your web site while searching the web may have ordered, but instead of ordering online, they called your company and placed an order by phone and the credit for the order went to a miscellaneous code.

This method of allocation is not perfect, but miscellaneous sales will be equitably redistributed.

Allocating miscellaneous/unknown orders is not a perfect representation. But, if you allocate orders on a weighted average basis, at least you know you made an equitable redistribution of orders and sales.

The series of Illustrations 8.2, 8.3, and 8.4 (on pages 102–105) reveals the impact of adjusting the orders and sales through redistribution of miscellaneous orders and is somewhat different from Illustration 8.1. Line 8, Orders Excluding Misc./Unk., totals all sources except miscellaneous orders. In this example, Columns H and I depict different percentages than those shown in Illustration 8.1. Why? In Illustration 8.1, the percentage of orders and sales was based on all orders and sales sources. In Illustration 8.2, the percentages are based on all orders and sales sources except Misc./Unk. sources. In Illustration 8.1, customers represented 60.1 percent of orders, whereas in Illustration 8.2, customers now represent 67.7 percent of orders (H-1). The 67.7 percent figure is calculated by dividing 182,909 orders (D-1) by 270,175 orders (excluding Misc./Unk.) from D-8.

Illustration 8.2

A	B	C	D	E
Line	Item	Circulation	Orders	% Response
1	Customers	2,438,793	182,909	7.50%
2	Prospecting	5,093,992	34,639	0.68%
3	Inserts	10,000,000	2,532	0.03%
4	Space Ads	7,000,000	7,147	0.10%
5	Web Orders		42,948	
6	Misc./Unknown		34,293	
7	**Total All Sources**		**304,468**	
8	Orders Excluding Misc./Unk.		270,175	

F	G	H	I
Average Order	Sales	Orders % of Total	Sales % of Total
$87.42	$15,989,946	67.70%	74.66%
$64.82	$2,245,284	12.82%	10.48%
$54.46	$137,884	0.94%	0.64%
$56.29	$402,305	2.65%	1.88%
$61.49	$2,640,873	15.90%	12.33%
$63.93	$2,192,351	0.00%	0.00%
$77.54	**$23,608,643**	**100.00%**	**100.00%**
	$21,416,292		

In Illustration 8.3, Column J, we detail how many of the miscellaneous orders are allocated elsewhere. J-1 shows that we will allocate 23,216 of the 34,293 miscellaneous orders (J-7) to customers. The 23,216 number is calculated by taking 34,293 miscellaneous orders multiplied by 67.7 percent (Illustration 8.2, H-1). Adding the 182,909 orders from D-1 in Illustration 8.2 to 23,216 orders from J-1 in Illustration 8.3, we now have total adjusted customer orders of 206,125 (K-1). Our response rate adjusts from 7.5 percent (E-1 in Illustration 8.2) to 8.45 percent (M-1 in Illustration 8.3), or an increase of 12.7 percent (L-1). Please note: Allocations in Column J are based on full decimal points. If you use the percentages expressed with two decimal points in Illustration 8.2, allocations in Illustration 8.3, Column J, will round somewhat differently than shown.

Illustration 8.3

A	B	J	K	L	M
Line	Item	Misc. Orders Allocated	Total Adjusted Orders	Increased Order %	Adjusted % Resp.
1	Customers	23,216	206,125	12.7%	8.45%
2	Prospecting	4,397	39,036	12.7%	0.77%
3	Inserts	322	2,854	12.7%	0.03%
4	Space Ads	907	8,054	12.7%	0.12%
5	Web Orders	5,451	48,399	12.7%	n/a
6	Misc./Unknown				
7	Total All Sources	34,293	304,468	0.00%	
8	Orders Excluding Misc./Unk.				

Allocating Sales

We undertake the same exercise for allocating sales. Percentages as shown in Illustration 8.2, Column I, are rounded to two decimal points, however, exact calculations in Illustration 8.4, Column O, are based on full decimals. Of the $2,192,351 in miscellaneous sales in Illustration 8.2, G-6, we will allocate 74.66253 percent (shown as 74.66 percent) of miscellaneous sales to customers (Illustration 8.2, I-1), or $1,636,865 (Illustration 8.4, N-1). Adjusted sales are now $17,626,811 (Illustration 8.4, O-1). Average order size is adjusted, as well, in Column Q in Illustration 8.4. In the case of customers, the average order for customers actually shrinks from $87.42 (Illustration 8.2, F-1) to $85.52 (Illustration 8.4, Q-1). Why? Because the miscellaneous average order sizes were smaller than customer orders. You could make the argument, then, that most miscellaneous orders tend to come from prospecting efforts, which is likely the case. But since there is no way to know for sure, it is more defendable to assume an "across all" marketing categories weighted average of all orders and sales.

Illustration 8.4

A	B	N	O	P	Q
Line	Item	Misc. Sales Allocated	Adjusted Sales	Increased Order %	Adjusted Avg. Order
1	Customers	$1,636,865	$17,626,811	10.2%	$85.52
2	Prospecting	$229,846	$2,475,130	10.2%	$63.41
3	Inserts	$14,115	$151,999	10.2%	$53.26
4	Space Ads	$41,183	$443,488	10.2%	$55.06
5	Web Orders	$270,342	$2,911,215	10.2%	$60.15
6	Misc./Unknown				
7	**Total All Sources**	**$2,192,351**	**$23,608,643**	**0.00%**	**$77.54**
8	Orders Excluding Misc./Unk.				

All orders and sales numbers for prospecting, inserts, space ads, and web orders are adjusted, too, using the same methodology.

Allocating miscellaneous orders increased prospecting orders from 34,639 (Illustration 8.2, D-2) to 39,036 (Illustration 8.3, K-2), or 12.7 percent (Illustration 8.3, L-2). The percent response rate increased from 0.68 percent (Illustration 8.2, E-2) to 0.77 percent (Illustration 8.3, M-2) or an increase of 12.7 percent (Illustration 8.3, L-2). Sales increased from $2,245,284 (Illustration 8.2, G-2) to $2,475,130 (Illustration 8.4, O-2), or an increase of 10.2 percent (Illustration 8.4, P-2).

You can also adjust individual prospecting mailing lists.

Making these adjustments on the macro basis is just the beginning. You should carry through these same allocations to individual customer database segments, individual prospecting mailing lists, insert media, magazine space ads, web order codes, etc.

You need to know where to allocate miscellaneous orders to help you mail prospects as aggressively as possible.

As will be demonstrated in the next chapter, Circulation Analysis, it is important to adjust all numbers to accurately evaluate individual results. For instance, increasing the prospecting orders by 12.7 percent and sales 10.2 percent for each individual list will now move some unprofitable lists into the profitable column. When evaluating what you will do during your next marketing effort, it can mean the difference between retaining certain mailing lists or dropping them entirely. And, if your objective is to grow your customer list, it follows that you'll want to mail as aggressively as possible to build your customer list. Therefore, you need to know how many of these miscellaneous orders can be credited to all your marketing efforts.

The Hennerberg Analytic Cycle

This flow chart represents the progression and relationships of the principals detailed in this book. The responsible Marketing Portfolio Manager never stops moving through the cycle, continually gathering more data, refining offers, initiating further testing, improving response rates.

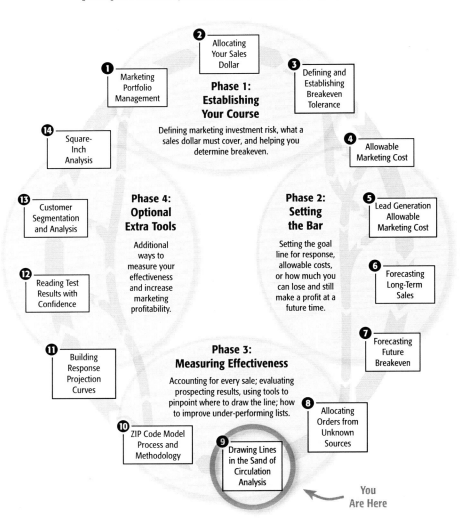

1 Marketing Portfolio Management

2 Allocating Your Sales Dollar

3 Defining and Establishing Breakeven Tolerance

Phase 1: Establishing Your Course

Defining marketing investment risk, what a sales dollar must cover, and helping you determine breakeven.

4 Allowable Marketing Cost

14 Square-Inch Analysis

13 Customer Segmentation and Analysis

Phase 4: Optional Extra Tools

Additional ways to measure your effectiveness and increase marketing profitability.

Phase 2: Setting the Bar

Setting the goal line for response, allowable costs, or how much you can lose and still make a profit at a future time.

5 Lead Generation Allowable Marketing Cost

12 Reading Test Results with Confidence

6 Forecasting Long-Term Sales

7 Forecasting Future Breakeven

11 Building Response Projection Curves

Phase 3: Measuring Effectiveness

Accounting for every sale; evaluating prospecting results, using tools to pinpoint where to draw the line; how to improve under-performing lists.

8 Allocating Orders from Unknown Sources

10 ZIP Code Model Process and Methodology

9 Drawing Lines in the Sand of Circulation Analysis

You Are Here

Chapter 9

Drawing Lines in the Sand of Circulation Analysis

When it comes time to evaluate individual mailing list performance, understanding where to draw the line in the circulation analysis is essential. When you are evaluating performance of several mailing lists and you sort them by best to poorest performance, it's likely that somewhere you "draw a line in the sand" where you choose to mail lists "above the line" and discontinue mailing lists "below the line." This chapter is all about helping you determine the most optimum place for you to draw your line. Draw it too high, and you may stop mailing lists that actually were helping you expand your new customer base. Draw it too low, and you'll lose money.

Draw your line too high, and you risk losing opportunity to grow. Draw it too low, and you'll lose money.

The foundation of performing a circulation analysis correctly is set by numbers established in your long-term value and future breakeven models, and allocation of miscellaneous orders. As described in the previous chapter, allocating miscellaneous orders is important if you want to mail as aggressively as possible to add new customers.

Your company's marketing reports may provide you with much of the data you need to evaluate individual list performance, but chances are you'll need to export that data into a spreadsheet or other database program. You then have the ability to add columns and calculations, and sort the data into meaningful ways so it can be properly analyzed.

Whether the reports are from your company's order processing database or you've exported it into a spreadsheet, generally, you'll need to have the following information:

A. List key code

B. List name

C. List segment or selection. Often you will want to mail specific selections of a list (recency—that is, how recently the names responded, such as 30- or 60-day buyers, or demographic data, for example) and give each list segment its own key code.

D. Quantity mailed, or circulation

E. Orders

F. Percent return, also known as response rate

G. Sales

H. Average order

I. Sales per thousand

J. Cost of goods sold (probably stated as a percentage of sales)

K. Fulfillment (probably stated as a percentage of sales)

L. Overhead (if you must allocate a percentage of overhead to prospecting)

M. Mailing cost (including printing, list rental, postage and related production expenses). Creative costs often are budgeted separately, but you have the option to distribute creative on a cost-per-thousand basis.

N. Profit contribution (or loss)

O. Profit contribution (or loss) per thousand mailed

P. Profit contribution (or loss) per piece mailed (can replace the per thousand mailed column)

Once you have the information in a spreadsheet and have populated the fields with live data, you can sort the data based on any criteria you choose. Illustration 9.1, on pages 114–115, shows all data in a spreadsheet sorted by key code. Using key codes (sorted lowest to highest) is often how computer reports are generated, but it makes examining the numbers on an individual list basis difficult and doesn't reveal trends or places to "draw a line in the sand." It also is the basis for expanding into Illustrations 9.2, 9.3 and 9.4 (described in a moment). A logical way to sort the data of each list or medium is from the highest profit contribution per thousand mailed to the lowest.

Sort profit contribution per list from highest to lowest.

Three Analysis Levels

There are three analysis levels by which you can choose to evaluate your circulation performance:

1. Conservative. Using strictly individual list performance without allocating miscellaneous/ unknown sales. This is the most conservative of approaches, as shown in Illustration 9.2 on pages 118–119.

2. Moderate. Adding in an allocation of miscellaneous/unknown sales to each list on a weighted average basis. As indicated in Chapter 8, we were able to increase our orders by 12.7 percent and sales by 10.2 percent. These increases enable you

to somewhat expand your prospecting on a list-by-list basis.

3. Aggressive. In addition to miscellaneous/unknown allocations, when you use cumulative circulation and sales as a basis for analysis, you will dramatically expand your circulation potential. As you will discover later in this chapter, this approach leverages two elements outside of traditional prospecting analysis that permit important adjustments to the numbers: a) using orders and sales from miscellaneous/unknown sources and b) averaging in your best lists with poorer lists to move your "line in the sand" deeper in your circulation plan so you can mail more volume, yet still retain an acceptable future breakeven.

The aggressive scenario isn't for everyone, but it is the fastest way to grow your customer file, yet manage risk.

Whether to use the conservative, moderate or most aggressive approach to circulation analysis is a decision you should make after reviewing the numbers. Even if you're not sure which position is best suited for your organization, you should run your circulation analysis under all three scenarios. Once you see your numbers sliced and diced three different ways, you can make a more informed decision based upon your level of comfort. The most aggressive approach (using miscellaneous/unknown order allocations and cumulative orders and sales) may not be for everyone. But for marketers who are more aggressive in their desire to grow, using the aggressive approach is a calculated way to analyze prospects and know where to draw your line in the sand of your circulation plan.

Example Circulation Analysis Illustrations

The four illustrations at the end of this chapter walk you through a progression of steps that illustrate circulation analysis. The Illustrations are:

Illustration 9.1

> Circulation analysis without miscellaneous and unknown sales allocated—sorted by key code

> This Illustration, on page 114–115, shows that when the data is sorted in key code order (often how data is presented), it is difficult to see any specific trends. In this example, there are 154 lists that were mailed with a total circulation of 5,093,992 (E-155), orders of 34,639 (F-155), a 0.68 percent response (G-155) and sales of $2,245,264 (H-155). After taking out cost of goods sold (COGS) (37 percent of sales), fulfillment (19 percent) and marketing cost (variable depending upon the list), there was a loss of $1,206,922 (P-155). These Illustrations all assume no overhead allocation. Overall loss per thousand mailed was $237.

In the following Illustrations 9.1–9.4, rows have been removed, so you can see the top, a mid-section, and bottom-line numbers.

Illustration 9.1

Line	Key Code	List Nm / Seg-mnt	Quantity	Orders	Pct	Sales	Average Order	Sales Per M	COGS (at 37%)	Fulfill-ment (at 19%)
1	1		22,029	164	0.74%	$9,232	$56.32	$419	$3,416	$1,754
2	2		22,029	183	0.83%	$10,671	$58.37	$484	$3,948	$2,027
3	3		44,058	247	0.56%	$15,672	$63.53	$356	$5,799	$2,978
4	4		44,058	258	0.58%	$17,813	$69.17	$404	$6,591	$3,384
5	5		22,029	153	0.69%	$10,026	$65.49	$455	$3,709	$1,905
6	6		22,029	136	0.62%	$8,325	$61.27	$378	$3,080	$1,582
7	7		17,623	161	0.91%	$8,146	$50.54	$462	$3,014	$1,548
8	8		55,072	387	0.70%	$22,496	$58.09	$408	$8,324	$4,274
9	9		110,145	883	0.80%	$52,813	$59.81	$479	$19,541	$10,035
10	10		22,029	167	0.76%	$11,738	$70.46	$533	$4,343	$2,230
73	73		12,933	108	0.83%	$10,556	$98.11	$816	$3,906	$2,006
74	74		14,528	110	0.76%	$8,955	$81.53	$616	$3,313	$1,701
75	75		15,407	95	0.62%	$5,378	$56.42	$349	$1,990	$1,022
76	76		13,603	110	0.81%	$6,957	$63.34	$511	$2,574	$1,322
77	77		14,436	90	0.62%	$4,905	$54.56	$340	$1,815	$932
78	78		17,658	32	0.18%	$3,357	$104.71	$190	$1,242	$638
79	79		21,725	26	0.12%	$3,836	$148.11	$177	$1,419	$729
80	80		31,797	38	0.12%	$4,187	$110.48	$132	$1,549	$796
81	81		21,447	24	0.11%	$1,504	$62.80	$70	$557	$286
82	82		30,052	61	0.20%	$4,490	$73.78	$149	$1,661	$853
83	83		15,713	86	0.55%	$4,760	$55.20	$303	$1,761	$904
146	146		25,364	156	0.61%	$8,744	$56.13	$345	$3,235	$1.661
147	147		16,070	71	0.44%	$4,302	$60.60	$268	$1,592	$817
148	148		20,731	131	0.63%	$8,652	$85.81	$417	$3,201	$1,644
149	149		20,751	106	0.51%	$5,221	$49.19	$252	$1,932	$992
150	150		20,731	83	056%	$4,421	$53.39	$300	$1,636	$840
151	151		34.944	286	0.82%	$18,721	$65.56	$536	$6,927	$3,557
152	152		38,249	259	0.68%	$16,169	$62.54	$423	$5,982	$3,072
153	153		13,792	94	0.68%	$7,076	$75.59	$513	$2,618	$1,344
154	154		21,401	186	0.87%	$9.874	$53.22	$461	$3,653	$1,876
155	TTL		5,093,992	34,639	0.68%	$2,245,264	$64.82	$441	$830,748	$426,600

M	N	O	P	Q
Ovr-hd (at 0%)	Mailing Cost	Mail-ing Cost/ M	Profit Contrib	Profit/ M
	$10,055	$456	$(5,993)	$(272)
	$10,221	$464	$(5,526)	$(251)
	$20,110	$456	$(13,214)	$(300)
	$19,495	$442	$(11,657)	$(265)
	$10,008	$454	$(5,597)	$(254)
	$10,008	$454	$(6,345)	$(288)
	$8,025	$455	$(4,441)	$(252)
	$24,546	$446	$(14,648)	$(266)
	$48,738	$442	$(25,500)	$(232)
	$9,889	$449	$(4,725)	$(214)
	$5,889	$455	$(1,245)	$(96)
	$6,616	$455	$(2,675)	$(184)
	$7,016	$455	$(4,650)	$(302)
	$6,194	$455	$(3,133)	$(230)
	$6,574	$455	$(4,415)	$(306)
	$8,041	$455	$(6,564)	$(372)
	$10,836	$498	$(9,139)	$(421)
	$15,068	$474	$(13,226)	$(416)
	$9,658	$450	$(8,997)	$(419)
	$12,136	$404	$(10,160)	$(338)
	$7,847	$499	$(5,753)	$(366)
	$10,760	$424	$(6,913)	$(273)
	$6,869	$427	$(4,976)	$(310)
	$7,927	$382	$(4,120)	$(199)
	$7,756	$374	$(5,459)	$(263)
	$6,088	$413	$(4,143)	$(281)
	$14,224	$407	$(5,987)	$(171)
	$16,021	$419	$(8,907)	$(233)
	$5,659	$410	$(2,545)	$(185)
	$8,458	$395	$(4,114)	$(192)
	$2,194,838	$431	$(1,206,922)	$(237)

Data sorted by key code, as shown here, is not helpful, and allows no intuitive analysis of the numbers.

Rows 11–72 are not shown, so you can see top and a mid-section.

Rows 84--145 are not shown, so you can see mid-section and bottom-line numbers.

Illustration 9.2:

Conservative Approach: Circulation analysis without miscellaneous and unknown sales allocated—sorted by highest to lowest performing list

Here, as shown on pages 118–119, the lists are sorted by best performing list, on a profit contribution per thousand basis, to the poorest performing list.

In Chapter 7—Determining Future Breakeven, the acceptable future breakeven point was calculated as a loss of $174.00 per thousand in the initial acquisition. If you were to strictly mail only those lists performing at a loss of $174.00 or better, your indicated future circulation would be just 996,208 (E-35). Of note, within this group of lists, the average loss per thousand is $127.00 (Q-35), above the acceptable future breakeven threshold loss of $174.00 in the initial acquisition. When you draw your line here, you are taking a conservative line on future prospecting. If you follow this direction, you drop your circulation from more than 5 million to just under 1 million, a dramatic drop that has a negative long-term impact on your business. However, if your organization is in a season of retrenching, this type of Draconian circulation cut may be indicated.

Illustration 9.2

A	B	C/D	E	F	G	H	I	J	K	L
Line	Key Code	List Nm / Seg-mnt	Quantity	Ord w/ 12.7% Misc & Unk Aloc	Pct Rtrn	Sales	Avg. Order	Sales per M	COGS (at 37%)	Ful-fill-ment (at 19%)
1	63		26,708	432	1.62%	$31,042	$71.90	$1,162	$11,486	$5,898
2	59		9,301	170	1.83%	$9,577	$56.34	$1,030	$3,544	$1,820
3	52		11,061	124	1.12%	$10,482	$84.37	$948	$3,878	$1,992
4	39		11,475	119	1.04%	$10,489	$88.00	$914	$3,881	$1,993
5	29		29,550	362	1.23%	$24,045	$66.36	$814	$8,897	$4,569
6	50		21,033	218	1.04%	$15,926	$73.04	$757	$5,893	$3,026
7	46		53,237	559	1.05%	$33,725	$60.38	$633	$12,478	$6,408
8	73		12,933	108	0.83%	$10,556	$98.11	$816	$3,906	$2,006
9	66		48,638	472	0.97%	$33,668	$71.32	$692	$12,457	$6,397
10	51		35,550	380	1.07%	$24,026	$63.20	$676	$8.889	$4,565
27	145		11,790	102	0.86%	$6,800	$66.85	$577	$2,516	$1,292
28	124		54,385	510	0.94%	$32,158	$63.06	$591	$11,898	$6,110
29	108		18,553	196	1.06%	$12,506	$63.70	$674	$4,627	$2,376
30	33		35,555	304	0.86%	$19,235	$63.18	$541	$7,117	$3,655
31	26		20,201	158	0.78%	$11,044	$69.68	$547	$4,086	$2,098
32	142		21,412	148	0.69%	$11,701	$79.23	$546	$4,329	$2,223
33	151		34,944	286	0.82%	$18,721	$65.56	$536	$6,927	$3,557
34	130		20,989	180	0.86%	$11,617	$64.50	$553	$4,298	$2,207
35	TOTAL		996,208	9,511	0.95%	$643,383	$67.65	$646	$238,052	$122,243
36			Lists above this line breakeven at ($174/M), in the example							
37	67		43,485	340	0.78%	$22,300	$65.66	$513	$8,251	$4,237
148	102		26,741	121	0.45%	$6,227	$51.59	$233	$2,304	$1,183
149	109		34,773	129	0.37%	$7,721	$59.93	$222	$2,857	$1,467
150	100		29,479	111	0.38%	$6,354	$57.30	$216	$2,351	$1,207
151	105		26,272	62	0.23%	$3,447	$55.98	$131	$1,275	$655
152	80		31,797	38	0.12%	$4,187	$110.48	$132	$1,549	$796
153	81		21,447	24	0.11%	$1,504	$62.80	$70	$557	$286
154	79		21,725	26	0.12%	$3,836	$148.11	$177	$1,419	$729
155	92		30,435	68	0.22%	$4,174	$61.31	$137	$1,544	$793
156	103		29,276	68	0.23%	$4,269	$63.19	$146	$1,580	$811
157	Total		5,093,992	34,639	0.68%	$2,245,264	$64.82	$441	$830,748	$426,600

M	N	O	P	Q
Ovr-hd (at 0%)	Mailing Cost	Mail-ing Cost/ M	Profit Contrib	Profit/ M
	$10,785	$404	$2,873	$108
	$3,756	$404	$458	$49
	$4,467	$404	$145	$13
	$4,585	$400	$31	$3
	$12,218	$413	$(1,638)	$(55)
	$8,494	$404	$(1,486)	$(71)
	$19,669	$369	$(4,830)	$(91)
	$5,889	$455	$(1,245)	$(96)
	$19,641	$404	$(4,827)	$(99)
	$14,356	$404	$(3,785)	$(106)
	$4,875	$413	$(1,883)	$(160)
	$22,897	$421	$(8,747)	$(161)
	$8,560	$461	$(3,057)	$(165)
	$14,358	$404	$(5,894)	$(166)
	$8,288	$410	$(3,428)	$(170)
	$8,785	$410	$(3,636)	$(170)
	$14,224	$407	$(5,987)	$(171)
	$8,769	$418	$(3,657)	$(174)
	$409,220	**$411**	**$(126,132)**	**$(127)**

in Chapter 7, Determining Future Breakeven

M	N	O	P	Q
	$17,560	$404	$(7,748)	$(178)
	$13,182	$493	$(10,442)	$(391)
	$17,478	$503	$(14,081)	$(405)
	$14,849	$504	$(12,053)	$(409)
	$12,415	$473	$(10,898)	$(415)
	$15,068	$474	$(13,226)	$(416)
	$9,658	$450	$(8,997)	$(419)
	$10,826	$498	$(9,139)	$(421)
	$14,648	$481	$(12,812)	$(421)
	$14,338	$490	$(12,460)	$(426)
	$2,194,838	**$431**	**$(1,206,922)**	**$(237)**

Rows 11–26 are not shown, so you can see top and a mid-section.

Rows 38–147 are not shown, so you can see mid-section and bottom-line numbers.

Direct Marketing Quantified: *The Knowledge is in the Numbers*

Illustration 9.3:

Moderate: Circulation analysis with miscellaneous and unknown sales allocated

This Illustration, on pages 122–123, goes to
the next step of allocating miscellaneous and
unknown orders using the percentages from
the example in Chapter 8. In this case, orders
were increased by 12.7 percent and sales were
increased by 10.2 percent.

After factoring in miscellaneous and unknown
orders, our mailable universe, that is, those lists
losing $174.00 per thousand or less, increased
to 1,324,020 (Illustration 9.3, E-45). The average
loss per thousand is now $114.00 per thousand
mailed (Q-45).

Even with adding back miscellaneous/unknown
orders and sales, the analysis would suggest that
you mail only 44 out of the 154 lists mailed, or
1.3 million out of 5 million initially mailed. You
would drop more than 3.7 million of your mail
volume viewing the results in this way.

Illustration 9.3

A	B	C/D	E	F	G	H	I	J	K	L
Line	Key Code	List Nm / Seg-mnt	Quantity	Ord w/ 12.7% Misc & Unk Aloc	Pct Rtrn	Sales w/ 10.2% Misc & Unk Alloc	Avg Ordr w/ Misc & Unk Alloc	Sls/M w/ Misc & Unk Alloc	COGS (at 37%)	Ful-fill-ment (at 19%)
1	63		26,708	487	1.82%	$34,220	$70.33	$1,281	$12,661	$6,502
2	59		9,301	192	2.06%	$10,558	$55.11	$1,135	$3,906	$2,006
3	52		11,061	140	1.27%	$11,555	$82.53	$1,045	$4,275	$2,195
4	39		11,475	134	1.17%	$11,563	$86.09	$1,008	$4,278	$2,197
5	29		29,550	408	1.38%	$26,507	$64.92	$897	$9,808	$5,036
6	50		21,033	246	1.17%	$17,556	$71.45	$835	$6,496	$3,336
7	73		12,933	121	0.94%	$11,637	$95.97	$900	$4,306	$2,211
8	46		53,237	629	1.18%	$37,177	$59.06	$698	$13,756	$7,064
9	66		46,638	532	1.09%	$37,115	$69.77	$763	$13,733	$7,052
10	51		35,550	428	1.21%	$26,485	$61.82	$745	$9,799	$5,032
38	153		13,792	105	0.76%	$7,800	$73.94	$566	$2,886	$1,481
39	69		82,567	715	0.87%	$45,377	$63.48	$550	$16,790	$8,622
40	53		11,548	112	0.97%	$7,797	$69.87	$675	$2,885	$1,481
41	95		14,118	93	0.66%	$7,712	$82.65	$546	$2,853	$1,465
42	154		21,401	209	0.98%	$10,885	$52.06	$509	$4,027	$2,068
43	143		62,586	468	0.75%	$31,522	$67.35	$504	$11,663	$5,989
44	72		23,196	194	0.84%	$12,111	$62.48	$522	$4,481	$2,301
45	TOTAL		1,324,020	13,454	1.02%	$888,599	$66.05	$671	$328,782	$168,834
46	Lists above this line, including misc./unk. allocation, breakeven at ($174/M)									
47	140		21,115	148	0.70%	$10,082	$68.05	$477	$3,730	$1,916
48	18		123,686	895	0.72%	$63,940	$71,48	$517	$23,658	$12,149
148	102		26,741	136	0.51%	$6,865	$50.47	$257	$2,540	$1,304
149	109		34,773	145	0.42%	$8,511	$58.62	$245	$3,149	$1,617
150	100		29,479	125	0.42%	$7,005	$56.05	$238	$2,592	$1,331
151	105		26,272	69	0.26%	$3,800	$54.76	$145	$1,406	$722
152	80		31,797	43	0.13%	$4,616	$108.07	$145	$1,708	$877
153	79		21,725	29	0.13%	$4,228	$144.88	$195	$1,564	$803
154	92		30,435	77	0.25%	$4,601	$59.98	$151	$1,702	$874
155	81		21,447	27	0.13%	$1,658	$61.43	$77	$614	$315
156	103		29,276	76	0.26%	$4,706	$61.81	$161	$1,741	$894
157	Total		5,093,992	39,036	0.77%	$2,475,130	$63.41	$486	$915,798	$470,275

M	N	O	P	Q
Ovr-hd (at 0%)	Mailing Cost	Mail-ing Cost/ M	Profit Contrib	Profit/ M
	$10,785	$404	$4,272	$160
	$3,756	$404	$890	$96
	$4,467	$404	$618	$56
	$4,585	$400	$503	$44
	$12,218	$413	$(555)	$(19)
	$8,494	$404	$(769)	$(37)
	$5,889	$455	$(769)	$(59)
	$19,669	$369	$(3,311)	$(62)
	$19,641	$404	$(3,310)	$(68)
	$14,346	$404	$(2,703)	$(76)
	$5,659	$410	$(2,226)	$(161)
	$33,342	$404	$(13,376)	$(162)
	$5,308	$460	$(1,877)	$(163)
	$5,701	$404	$(2,308)	$(163)
	$8,458	$395	$(3,669)	$(171)
	$24,736	$395	$(10,867)	$(174)
	$9,367	$404	$(4,039)	$(174)
	$542,055	**$409**	**$(151,072)**	**$(114)**
	$8,141	$386	$(3,705)	$(175)
	49,947	$404	$(21,814)	$(176)
	$13,182	$493	$(10,162)	$(380)
	$17,478	$503	$(13,733)	$(395)
	$14,849	$504	$(11,767)	$(399)
	$12,415	$473	$(10,743)	$(409)
	$15,068	$474	$(13,037)	$(410)
	$10,826	$498	$(8,966)	$(413)
	$14,648	$481	$(12,624)	$(415)
	$9,658	$450	$(8,929)	$(416)
	$14,338	$490	$(12,267)	$(419)
	$2,194,838	**$431**	**$(1,105,781)**	**$(217)**

Rows 11–37 are not shown, so you can see top and a mid-section.

Rows 49--147 are not shown, so you can see mid-section and bottom-line numbers.

Illustration 9.4:

Aggressive: Circulation analysis with miscellaneous and unknown allocations based on cumulative results

This Illustration, on pages 126–127, takes us to a different perspective on evaluating which lists to mail in the future. When we accumulate the Cumulative Quantity mailed (Column R), Cumulative Sales (Column S), Cumulative Profit Contribution (Column T), and average the Cumulative Profit per Thousand (Column U), our view of prospecting changes dramatically.

We now can mail 3,501,976 circulation yielding 30,067 new customers (E-101) and know that these new customers will breakeven at an acceptable future date. This still cuts circulation considerably (from 5 million to 3.5 million), but the poorest performing 1.5 million circulation was producing new customers that may never breakeven.

In Illustration 9.4, on pages 126–127, rows 11–92 and 104–147 are not shown, so you can see top, mid-section, and bottom-line numbers.

Illustration 9.4

A	B	C/D	E	F	G	H	I	J	K	L
Line	Key Code	List Nm / Seg- mnt	Quantity	Ord w/ 12.7% Misc & Unk Aloc	Pct Rtrn	Sales w/ 10.2% Misc & Unk Alloc	Avg Ordr w/ Misc & Unk Alloc	Sls/M w/ Misc & Unk Alloc	COGS (at 37%)	Ful- fill- ment (at 19%)
1	63		26,708	487	1.82%	$34,220	$70.33	$1,281	$12,661	$6,502
2	59		9,301	192	2.06%	$10,558	$55.11	$1,135	$3,906	$2,006
3	52		11,061	140	1.27%	$11,555	$82.53	$1,045	$4,275	$2,195
4	39		11,475	134	1.17%	$11,563	$86.09	$1,008	$4,278	$2,197
5	29		29,550	408	1.38%	$26,507	$64.92	$897	$9,808	$5,036
6	50		21,033	246	1.17%	$17,556	$71.45	$835	$6,496	$3,336
7	73		12,933	121	0.94%	$11,637	$95.97	$900	$4,306	$2,211
8	46		53,237	629	1.18%	$37,177	$59.06	$698	$13,756	$7,064
9	66		48,638	532	1.09%	$37,115	$69.77	$763	$13,733	$7,052
10	51		35,550	428	1.21%	$26,485	$61.82	$745	$9,799	$5,032
93	8		55,072	436	0.79%	$24,799	$56.82	$450	$9,176	$4,712
94	134		31,541	179	0.57%	$10,570	$59.18	$335	$3,911	$2,008
95	149		20,751	120	0.58%	$5,755	$48.12	$277	$2,129	$1,093
96	34		6,734	38	0.57%	$2,323	$60.38	$345	$860	$441
97	1		22,029	185	0.84%	$10,177	$55.10	$462	$3,765	$1,934
98	25		13,030	87	0.67%	$4,349	$49.86	$334	$1,609	$826
99	146		25,364	176	0.69%	$9,639	$54.90	$380	$3,567	$1,831
100	111		37,286	294	0.79%	$18,611	$63.22	$499	$6,886	$3,536
101	TOTAL		3,501,976	30,067	0.86%	$1,923,964	$63.99	$549	$711,867	$365,553
102			Lists above this line, including misc./unk. allocation and								
103	110		118,443	1,012	0.85%	$58,171	$57.47	$491	$21,523	$11,052
148	102		26,741	136	0.51%	$6,865	$50.47	$257	$2,540	$1,304
149	109		34,773	145	0.42%	$8,511	$58.62	$245	$3,149	$1,617
150	100		29,479	125	0.42%	$7,005	$56.05	$238	$2,592	$1,331
151	105		26,272	69	0.26%	$3,800	$54.76	$145	$1,406	$722
152	80		31,797	43	0.13%	$4,616	$108.07	$145	$1,708	$877
153	79		21,725	29	0.13%	$4,228	$144.88	$195	$1,564	$803
154	92		30,435	77	0.25%	$4,601	$59.98	$151	$1,702	$874
155	81		21,447	27	0.13%	$1,658	$61.43	$77	$614	$315
156	103		29,276	76	0.26%	$4,706	$61.81	$161	$1,741	$894
157	Total		5,093,992	39,036	0.77%	$2,475,130	$63.41	$486	$915,798	$470,275

M	N	O	P	Q	R	S	T	U
Ovr-hd (at 0%)	Mailing Cost	Mailing Cost/ M	Profit Contrib	Profit per M	Cumulative Qty Mailed	Cumulative Sales	Cumulative Profit Contrib	Cumulative Profit/ M
	$10,785	$404	$4,272	$160	26,708	$34.220	$4,272	$160
	$3,756	$404	$890	$96	36,008	$44,778	$5,161	$143
	$4,467	$404	$618	$56	47,069	$56,333	$5,779	$123
	$4,585	$400	$503	$44	58,544	$67,896	$6,282	$107
	$12,218	$413	$(555)	$(19)	88,094	$94,402	$5,726	$65
	$8,494	$404	$(769)	$(37)	109.127	$111,959	$4,957	$45
	$5,889	$455	$(769)	$(59)	122,060	$123,595	$4,188	$34
	$19,669	$369	$(3,311)	$(62)	175,297	$160,772	$877	$5
	$19,641	$404	$(3,310)	$(68)	223,935	$197,887	$(2,433)	$(11)
	$14,356	$404	$(2,703)	$(76)	259,485	$224,372	$(5,136)	$(20)
	$24,546	$446	$(13,635)	$(248)	3,345,241	$1,862,540	$(563,147)	$(168)
	$12,466	$395	$(7,815)	$(248)	3,376,782	$1,873,110	$(570,962)	$(169)
	$7,756	$374	$(5,224)	$(252)	3,397,533	$1,878,865	$(576,186)	$(170)
	$2,719	$404	$(1,697)	$(252)	3,404,267	$1,881,189	$(577,883)	$(170)
	$10,055	$456	$(5,577)	$(253)	3,426,296	$1,891,365	$(583,460)	$(170)
	$5,262	$404	$(3,348)	$(257)	3,439,326	$1,895,714	$(586,809)	$(171)
	$10,760	$424	$(6,519)	$(257)	3,464,690	$1,905,353	$(593,328)	$(171
	$17,780	$477	$(9,591)	$(257)	3,501,976	$1,923,964	$(602,919)	$(172)
	1,449,463	$414	$(602,919)	$(172)				
cumulative results, breakeven at ($174/M)								
	11,221	$404	$(6,529)	$(235)	3,053,344	$1,730,630	$(491,962)	$(161)
	$13,182	$493	$(10,162)	$(380)	4,868,788	$2,436,005	$(1,013,715)	$(208)
	$17,478	$503	$(13,733)	$(395)	4,903,561	$2,444,516	$(1,027,448)	$(210)
	$14,849	$504	$(11,767)	$(399)	4,933,040	$2,451,521	$(1,039,215)	$(211)
	$12,415	$473	$(10,743)	$(409)	4,959,311	$2,455,321	$(1,049,958)	$(212)
	$15,068	$474	$(13,037)	$(410)	4,991,108	$2,459,937	$(1,062,995)	$(213)
	$10,826	$498	$(8,966)	$(413)	5,012,833	$2,464,165	$(1,071,961)	$(214)
	$14,648	$481	$(12,624)	$(415)	5,043,268	$2,468,766	$(1,084,585)	$(215)
	$9,658	$450	$(8,929)	$(416)	5,064,715	$2,470,424	$(1,093,514)	$(216)
	$14,338	$490	$(12,267)	$(419)	5,093,992	$2,475,130	$(1,105,781)	$(217)
	$2,194,838	$431	$(1,105,781)	$(217)				

A summary of the three circulation analysis scenarios appears in Illustration 9.5 below. This summary illustrates how including allocated miscellaneous, unknown results and a weighted average of cumulative results can expand your circulation.

Actual quantity mailed was 5,093,992 with 34,639 orders and sales of $2,245,264. Using the aggressive circulation analysis approach, you can retain breakeven within the time frame you are comfortable with and still retain 69 percent of circulation and 86 percent of sales. So, by dropping 31 percent of your circulation, you only lose 14 percent of sales.

Illustration 9.5

A	B	C	D
Stance	**Quantity**	**Orders**	**Sales**
Conservative	996,208	9,511	$643,383
Moderate	1,324,020	13,454	$888,559
Aggressive	3,501,976	30,067	$1,923,964

Since no one likes to lose sales, even if those sales come at a very high cost, you should look at ways you can lift response from the under-performing lists to bring them into the acceptable profit (or loss) column.

One tool that is useful for lifting response rates is creation of a ZIP code model. With a ZIP code model, you can identify geographies on a ZIP code basis where you mail under-performing lists. By eliminating a substantial portion of poor performing ZIP codes, you often can lift response rates high enough to make them worthwhile to mail. The next chapter will describe how to create a ZIP code model.

E	F	G	H
Circulation Lost	Sales Lost	% Circulation Retained	% Sales Retained
4,097,784	$1,601,881	20%	29%
3,769,972	$1,356,705	26%	40%
1,592,016	$321,300	69%	86%

Effect of Allocating Sales and Using Cumulative Results to Expand Circulation Potential

The impact of combining the allocation of miscellaneous/unknown sales and the accumulated sales based on average circulation has a scalable impact on the volume of prospecting circulation.

Illustration 9.6

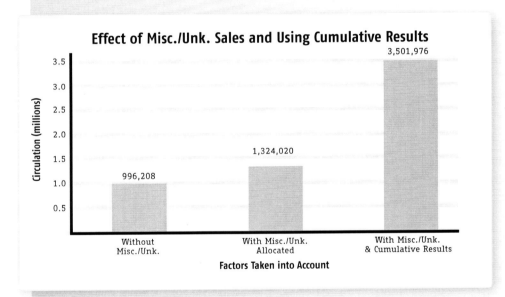

Effect of Misc./Unk. Sales and Using Cumulative Results

The Hennerberg Analytic Cycle

This flow chart represents the progression and relationships of the principals detailed in this book. The responsible Marketing Portfolio Manager never stops moving through the cycle, continually gathering more data, refining offers, initiating further testing, improving response rates.

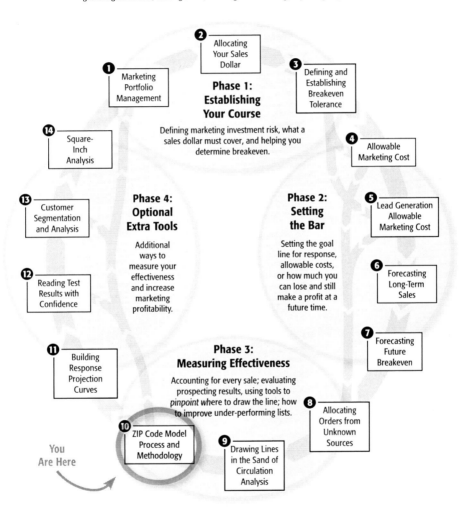

1 Marketing Portfolio Management

2 Allocating Your Sales Dollar

3 Defining and Establishing Breakeven Tolerance

4 Allowable Marketing Cost

5 Lead Generation Allowable Marketing Cost

6 Forecasting Long-Term Sales

7 Forecasting Future Breakeven

8 Allocating Orders from Unknown Sources

9 Drawing Lines in the Sand of Circulation Analysis

10 ZIP Code Model Process and Methodology

11 Building Response Projection Curves

12 Reading Test Results with Confidence

13 Customer Segmentation and Analysis

14 Square-Inch Analysis

Phase 1: Establishing Your Course

Defining marketing investment risk, what a sales dollar must cover, and helping you determine breakeven.

Phase 2: Setting the Bar

Setting the goal line for response, allowable costs, or how much you can lose and still make a profit at a future time.

Phase 3: Measuring Effectiveness

Accounting for every sale; evaluating prospecting results, using tools to *pinpoint* where to draw the line; how to improve under-performing lists.

Phase 4: Optional Extra Tools

Additional ways to measure your effectiveness and increase marketing profitability.

You Are Here

Chapter 10

ZIP Code Model Process and Methodology

Now that you know where to "draw the line" in circulation analysis, you may wonder what you can do to move some of those lists that fall "under the line," and maybe a few of the poorer lists that just sneak "over the line," to a more profitable position.

A ZIP code model is an inexpensive tool you can use to increase the profitability of a mailing list. Best of all, you can create a ZIP model using a spreadsheet.

The objective of using a ZIP code model is to lift response rates. There usually are ZIP codes that have much higher than average response rates that can be mailed more frequently; and conversely, there are ZIP codes at the bottom end of the spectrum that should be suppressed from mailing. You might choose to apply a ZIP model only to under-performing lists; on the other hand, you may choose to apply it to all lists that you mail to give your marketing efforts an overall lift.

A ZIP model is usually applied to lackluster performing lists for the purpose of lifting them to higher response rates.

In a ZIP code model, ZIP codes can be separated into deciles (10 equal groups of 10 percent of volume per group). If you mail 1,000,000 total names, 10 groups will represent 100,000 names per decile.

Alternatively, demi-deciles, 20 groups of 5 percent of volume, are most effective when your mail quantity is in the tens of millions or more. For example, if you mail 10,000,000, 20 equal groups of 5 percent of the total, or 500,000, would be mailed in each demi-decile.

With more than 42,000 ZIP codes in the U.S., the ability to segment ZIP codes is high. Unless you are mailing tens of millions of names, it's unlikely you are mailing all ZIP codes. In fact, you may be mailing only a small percentage of all ZIP codes in the country.

Afraid of losing sales if you suppress the bottom 10% of ZIP code circulation? You'll more than make it up by mailing the top 10% of ZIP circulation twice.

This model often reveals that ZIP codes in the top one or two deciles (10 percent or 20 percent) usually have a much better than average performance level, while the bottom one or two deciles often drag down average performance. It is common to discover that the bottom 10 percent of ZIP code circulation (representing 10 percent of your marketing cost) only produces 1 percent to 2 percent of your sales. Any concern about lost sales or circulation can be more than recovered by mailing the top deciles more frequently. The top 10 percent of circulation sometimes produces 20 percent to 30 percent or more of sales.

There are different approaches to creating ZIP code models. The steps outlined here are ones this author has successfully used for many years. This model can be created using a spreadsheet program on your PC.

Gathering Data

Information needed to create a ZIP code model should include data derived from a full year or a season. Information by individual ZIP code should include:

- ▶ ZIP code

- ▶ Circulation by ZIP code

- ▶ Number of Orders by ZIP code

- ▶ Sales by ZIP code

► City (or Post Office) and state for each ZIP code (helpful, but not critical)

Calculating and Sorting Data

After obtaining the data above, add headings to the spreadsheet and calculate percent response rate and sales per thousand for each ZIP code.

Next, sort the ZIP codes from highest sales per thousand to lowest sales per thousand.

Separating Responsive from Non-Responsive ZIP Codes

Don't be alarmed if you mailed 35,000 ZIP codes and discover that 25,000 of those codes had no response at all. Move all non-responsive ZIP codes to a different worksheet and only work with the ZIP codes from responsive ZIPs. Data from non-responsive ZIP codes will be analyzed separately. How to do that will be covered later in this chapter.

Dividing ZIPs into Deciles or Demi-Deciles

The determining factor of placing ZIP codes into the top decile, second decile, etc., is not based on dividing ZIP codes into 10 groups. That is, if you have 10,000 ZIP codes, you do *not* place the top 1,000 ZIP codes in the first decile, the next 1,000 ZIP codes in the second decile, etc.

The recommended methodology is to segment ZIP codes into deciles based on quantity mailed (or circulation). In your spreadsheet you will need to add a column for cumulative mail quantity. Now that "sales per thousand per ZIP code" is sorted from highest to lowest, you need to calculate the cumulative mail quantity.

In the example in Illustration 10.1, on pages 138–139, there were 1,876,747 names mailed to responsive ZIP codes in this prospecting effort. Therefore, to arrive at where to segment these ZIPs into deciles we divide the 1,876,747 total circulation into 10 equal groups. The target is to have 187,674 +/– circulation quantity per decile.

When you arrive at the ZIP code where the cumulative quantity is close to the target decile quantity — in this case, 187,674 — a line is drawn at that point to segment ZIP code deciles. ZIP codes above this point fall into decile one.

You continue with this same process, starting over on the cumulative quantity mailed until you reach a cumulative quantity of 187,674 (either under or over). You continue this process until all ZIP codes are classified into one of 10 deciles.

Within a decile, you now calculate that decile's total quantity, orders, sales, response rate, and the sales per thousand.

Next, summarize the data into a separate spreadsheet. In Illustration 10.1, the summary of 7,102 ZIP codes (Column C, Line 11) reveals that the top decile (based on the quantity mailed) has 2,023 ZIP codes (C-1). There were 3,381 orders from ZIP codes in this top decile (E-1), with a response rate of 1.80 percent (F-1) compared to the overage average of 0.69 percent (F-11). Decile 1 ZIPs respond at a rate that is 163 percent (G-1) higher than average. Decile 1 also features an average sales per thousand of $1,512 (I-1) that is nearly four times higher than average (I-11).

Clearly, the ZIP codes in decile 1 are highly desirable to mail.

At the other end of the scale is decile 10. Of the 187,451 names mailed, these ZIPs yielded only a 0.22 percent response rate (F-10) compared to the overall average of 0.69 percent (F-11). Sales per thousand of $62.00 (I-10) are significantly under the overall average of $410.00 (I-11).

One other important item to note is that there are 2,023 ZIP codes in decile 1. Decile 2 has 811 ZIP codes, and, in each decile, there are fewer and fewer ZIP codes. Yet, the cumulative quantity is still +/– the targeted 187,674 circulation per ZIP code. This is attributed to many ZIP codes with low circulation, but high response, that push the averages up. Be reminded again that ZIP codes with no response, which skew the low end of ZIP codes, have been removed. The method of deciding which of the unresponsive ZIP codes to mail will be described at the end of this chapter.

Illustration 10.1

A	B	C	D	E
Line	Decile	No. of Zips	Qty	Orders
1	1	2,023	187,572	3,381
2	2	811	187,924	1,820
3	3	664	187,486	1,516
4	4	601	187,680	1,333
5	5	583	187,685	1,198
6	6	556	187,865	1,002
7	7	509	187,598	882
8	8	503	187,853	742
9	9	476	187,633	604
10	10	376	187,451	404
11	Total	7,102	1,876,747	12,882

F	G	H	I	J
% Response	Change from Average	Sales	Average Sales	Change from Average
1.80%	163%	$283,564	$1,512	269%
0.97%	41%	$121,935	$649	58%
0.81%	18%	$89,750	$479	17%
0.71%	3%	$71,195	$379	-7%
0.64%	-7%	$57.899	$308	-25%
0.53%	-22%	$46,927	$250	-39%
0.47%	-32%	$37,350	$199	-51%
0.39%	-42%	$28,820	$153	-63%
0.32%	-53%	$20,503	$109	-73%
0.22%	-69%	$11,706	$62	-85%
0.69%	**0%**	**$769,648**	**$410**	**0%**

Having this summary by decile enables the creation of a chart to illustrate response rates for individual deciles compared to the response rates based on a cumulative average response rate. The following chart, Illustration 10.2, shows how deciles 1 through 4 performed above average, and how deciles 5 through 10 pulled down the overall average.

Illustration 10.2

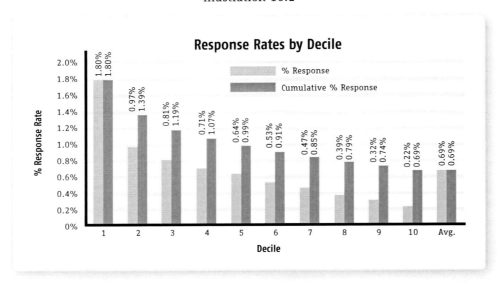

Response rates tell a lot of the story, but a more accurate measurement is using sales per thousand mailed. Illustration 10.3, opposite, illustrates a similar drop-off of sales per thousand when charted.

Having this data now enables you to know where you should decrease circulation based on the objective sales per thousand (or response) defined in your long-term sales value model and breakeven models.

If you need a small lift in results, you might choose to drop only deciles 9 and 10 from your mailing.

If you need a more dramatic lift to improve list performance, you might choose to drop off deciles 6 through 10. With the "Change from Average" identified in Illustration 10.1, you can accurately determine how many deciles should be dropped for each individual list.

Illustration 10.3

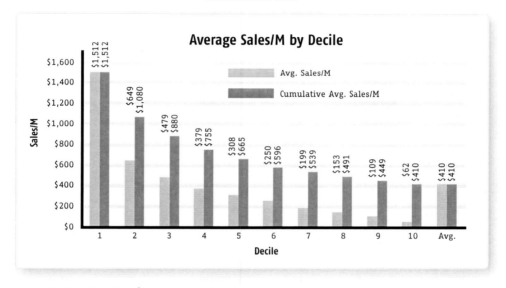

Sales by Decile

Perhaps a "bigger picture" view is to compare sales from each decile to determine the effect on your overall sales if you drop certain ZIP codes. If you were to drop decile 10, you would drop 10 percent of your circulation and lose 1.5 percent of your sales (Illustration 10.4, G-10, on pages 142–143). By dropping deciles 9 and 10, you would drop 20 percent of your circulation and lose 4.2 percent of sales (combination 2.7 percent in decile 9 and 1.5 percent in decile 10, G-9 and G-10).

Of course, you'd probably prefer not to lose 1.5 percent or 4.2 percent of sales, but chances are you can mail deciles 1 and 2 a second or even third time, and yield better results than mailing deciles 9 and 10 just once.

Illustration 10.4

A	B	C	D
Line	Decile	No. of Zips	Qty
1	1	2,023	187,572
2	2	811	187,924
3	3	664	187,486
4	4	601	187,680
5	5	583	187,685
6	6	556	187,865
7	7	509	187,598
8	8	503	187,853
9	9	476	187,633
10	10	376	187,451

Non-Responsive ZIPs

Earlier it was suggested to set non-responsive ZIP codes aside. The number of those ZIP codes is often astonishing.

Often thousands of ZIP codes are mailed only a handful of pieces of mail. Just because prospects in those ZIP codes did not respond does not mean they should be suppressed from future mailings. Remember, in decile 1 a very large number of ZIP codes were mailed only a few pieces of mail, but one prospect responded, catapulting that ZIP code into the top decile.

E	F	G	H	I
Cumu-lative Quantity	Sales	% Total Sales	Cumu-lative Sales	% Cumul Sales
187,572	$283,564	36.8%	$283,564	36.8%
375,496	$121,934	15.8%	$405,498	52.7%
562,982	$89,750	11.7%	$495,248	64.3%
750,662	$71,195	9.3%	$566,443	73.6%
938,347	$57,899	7.5%	$624,342	81.1%
1,126,212	$46,927	6.1%	$671,269	87.2%
1,313,810	$37,350	4.9%	$708,619	92.1%
1,501,663	$28,820	3.7%	$737,439	95.8%
1,689,296	$20,503	2.7%	$757,942	98.5%
1,876,747	$11,706	1.5%	$769,648	100.0%

One approach to evaluating non-responsive ZIP codes is to look at the average response rate you must generate from a ZIP code to breakeven. Let's say you need at least a 1.0 percent response. If that's the case, segment ZIP codes where you have mailed 100 or fewer pieces and code them "Unresponsive Low" ZIPs. Or if you need 0.50 percent or more, then draw the line at a quantity of 50 mailed per ZIP code. In either case, you should consider mailing those "Unresponsive Low" ZIP codes since if only one household responds, it will place that ZIP code in a high performing decile.

Again, using 1.0 percent as your benchmark, for any ZIPs where you have mailed 101 or more pieces, you probably should suppress those from mailings. If you require 0.50 percent, suppress those ZIP codes where you have mailed 51 or more pieces.

Illustration 10.5, below, illustrates the impact of non-responsive ZIP codes. In the case of this illustration, the assumption has been made that ZIP codes with 100 or fewer pieces mailed qualify as "Unresponsive Low" (UL). Those ZIP codes—25,571 of them (C-12)—will be mailed again, even though they represented 422,828 of the circulation. The circula-

Illustration 10.5

A	B	C	D	E
Line	Decile	No. of Zips	Qty	Orders
1	1	2,023	187,572	3,381
2	2	811	187,924	1,820
3	3	664	187,486	1,516
4	4	601	187,680	1,333
5	5	583	187,685	1,198
6	6	556	187,865	1,002
7	7	509	187,598	882
8	8	503	187,853	742
9	9	476	187,633	604
10	10	376	187,451	404
11	Sub-Total	7,102	1,876,747	12,882
12	UL	25,571	422,828	
13	UH	3,050	637,948	
14	**TOTAL**	**35,723**	**2,937,523**	**12,882**

"UL" ZIP codes are ZIPs with 100 or fewer mailed per ZIP code.

"UH" ZIP codes are ZIPs with 101 or more mailed per ZIP code.

tion of these UL ZIPs represented 14 percent of the circulation. If you need to pare down the ZIP codes further to more aggressively mail for profitability, change the quantity per ZIP code to a number you're more comfortable with mailing (for example, only mailing ZIPs with 50 or fewer quantity per ZIP code).

In this example, there were 3,050 "Unresponsive High" (UH) ZIP codes that accounted for 637,948 of the circulation, or nearly 22 percent of the volume (C-13, D-13). Omitting these ZIP codes from your mail program will enhance profitability tremendously.

F	G	H	I
% Response	Sales	Average Sales	Average Sales/M
1.80%	$283,564	$83.87	$1,511.76
0.97%	$121,935	$67.00	$648.85
0.81%	$89,750	$59.20	$478.70
0.71%	$71,195	$53.41	$379.34
0.64%	$57,899	$48.33	$308.49
0.53%	$46,927	$46.83	$249.79
0.47%	$37,350	$42.35	$199.10
0.39%	$28,820	$38.84	$153.42
0.32%	$20,503	$33.95	$109.27
0.22%	$11,706	$28.98	$62.45
0.69%	$769,649		
0.44%	$769,648	$59.75	$262.01

Back-End Applications of a ZIP Code Model

It isn't just response rates that have applications for ZIP code models. For instance, if you send a product on an approval basis, you might examine ZIP codes that have higher levels of bad debt and suppress them from mailings. You might evaluate performance by ZIP code for returned products, retention or other criteria. As you can see, ZIP models have other uses that will help make your business more profitable.

A ZIP model is a basic tool, not to be confused with advanced models.

There are many other types of models for analyzing and refining lists. They all have a place. A ZIP code model can't replace the power of an advanced model, such as CHAID or Logistic Regression. Rather, a ZIP model is a basic model that can be applied to most lists. Advanced models inherently apply many layers of criteria, some of which might include ZIP codes. You should not apply a ZIP code model to an advanced model, because that model should include people more likely to respond to your offer even if they reside in decile 10 ZIPs, for example. The advanced model enables you to mail those few individuals that you might otherwise miss.

The Hennerberg Analytic Cycle

This flow chart represents the progression and relationships of the principals detailed in this book. The responsible Marketing Portfolio Manager never stops moving through the cycle, continually gathering more data, refining offers, initiating further testing, improving response rates.

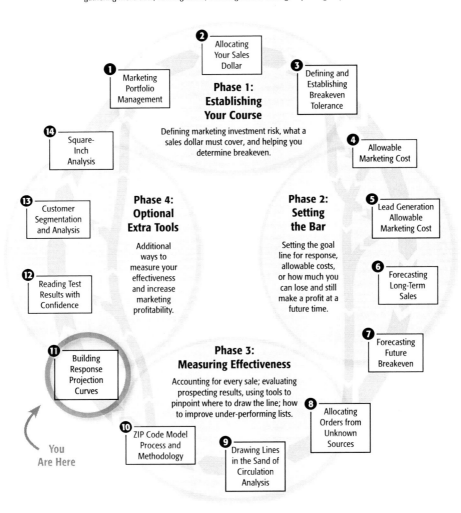

❶ Marketing Portfolio Management

❷ Allocating Your Sales Dollar

Phase 1: Establishing Your Course

Defining marketing investment risk, what a sales dollar must cover, and helping you determine breakeven.

❸ Defining and Establishing Breakeven Tolerance

❹ Allowable Marketing Cost

❺ Lead Generation Allowable Marketing Cost

❻ Forecasting Long-Term Sales

❼ Forecasting Future Breakeven

Phase 2: Setting the Bar

Setting the goal line for response, allowable costs, or how much you can lose and still make a profit at a future time.

❽ Allocating Orders from Unknown Sources

❾ Drawing Lines in the Sand of Circulation Analysis

Phase 3: Measuring Effectiveness

Accounting for every sale; evaluating prospecting results, using tools to pinpoint where to draw the line; how to improve under-performing lists.

❿ ZIP Code Model Process and Methodology

⓫ Building Response Projection Curves

You Are Here

⓬ Reading Test Results with Confidence

⓭ Customer Segmentation and Analysis

⓮ Square-Inch Analysis

Phase 4: Optional Extra Tools

Additional ways to measure your effectiveness and increase marketing profitability.

Chapter 11

Building Response Projection Curves

Response projection curves are valuable for the early reading of response rates to project the final performance of a mailing. If you happen to market in an environment where you need to quickly make a rollout decision based on a test, you especially need to establish a response curve.

Building a response curve requires patience and the accumulation of data over at least three different mail dates. To build the information, you need to know the date your mail was dropped and the total responses received, by day, following the drop.

Response curves are valuable to project response, especially when testing and you are eager to see results.

Illustration 11.1, on pages 152–153, uses detailed response data from three different mail dates with averages for those three. Columns B and C show the week and days from the mail date.

Columns D and E are responses by day from the first mail drop date. Columns F and G are from the second mail date and Columns H and I are from the third mail date.

Column J totals response from the three mailings, by day. Column K is the percentage of the total responses by day, or, what we consider the "percent complete."

This example illustrates that three weeks (15 business days) after a mail drop, 25 percent of the response has been received (K-15). The "doubling date," that is, the time when your response should be about 50 percent complete, happens 20 to 21 business days after the mail date (K-20 and K-21). It's at this point that you can look at your actual response from a mailing and double it to project about what you will receive over the next several weeks.

As Illustration 11.1, on pages 152–153, illustrates, after 60 business days it's likely you are 98 percent complete. Usually you can expect orders to trickle in for several weeks, months and sometimes years, after a marketing effort.

There are a few situations you should consider as you create a response curve. Your results can be influenced if you mail from different locations in the country. Another factor can be mailing on different days of the week. If you mail from the same location, and on the same day of the week, your response curve should give you a consistent view of your results.

Illustration 11.1

A	B	C	D	E	F	G
Line	Week	Business Days from Mail Date	Resp by Day from 1st Mailing	% Complete	Resp by Day from 2nd Mailing	% Complete
1	1	1				
2		2				
3		3				
4		4	41	0.2%	34	0.2%
5		5	54	0.3%	98	0.6%
6	2	6	85	0.4%	147	0.9%
7		7	105	0.5%	370	2.3%
8		8	220	1.1%	428	2.7%
9		9	291	1.5%	572	3.6%
10		10	356	1.8%	717	4.5%
12		12	2,062	10.4%	1,233	7.8%
13		13	2,801	14.1%	1,787	11.2%
14		14	3,244	16.3%	3,233	20.3%
15		15	3,892	19.6%	4,060	25.5%
16	4	16	4,812	24.2%	4,525	28.5%
17		17	4,983	25.1%	4,829	30.45
18		18	5,021	25.3%	5,844	36.7%
19		19	5,922	29.8%	7,329	46.1%
20		20	6,821	34.3%	8,644	54.4%
21	5	21	10,307	51.9%	9,234	58.1%
22		22	11,458	57.7%	9,888	62.2%
52		52	18,849	94.9%	15,244	95.9%
53		53	18,893	95.1%	15,291	96.1%
54		54	18,932	95.3%	15,302	96.2%
55		55	18,976	95.5%	15,404	96.9%
56	12	56	18,999	95.7%	15,588	98.0%
57		57	19,035	95.8%	15,595	98.1%
58		58	19,198	96.7%	15,602	98.1%
59		59	19,255	96.9%	15,633	98.3%
60		60	19,352	97.4%	15,652	98.4%
61	Final		19,869	100.0%	15,907	100.0%

H	I	J	K
Resp by Day from 3rd Mailing	% Complete	Total Resp by Day All 3 Mailings	Avg. % Complete
12	0.2%	87	0.2%
44	0.7%	196	0.5%
73	1.2%	305	0.7%
77	1.2%	552	1.3%
164	2.7%	812	1.9%
255	4.1%	1,118	2.7%
399	6.5%	1,472	3.5%
1,052	17.1%	4,347	10.4%
1,622	26.3%	6,210	14.8%
1,824	29.6%	8,301	19.8%
2,343	38.0%	10,295	24.6%
2,719	44.1%	12,056	28.8%
2,779	45.1%	12,287	29.3%
2,833	46.0%	13,698	32.7%
2,944	47.8%	16,195	38.6%
3,042	49.4%	18,507	44.1%
3,899	63.3%	19,541	54.6%
4,044	65.6%	25,390	60.6%
6,010	97.5%	40,103	95.6%
6,012	97.5%	40,196	95.8%
6,033	97.9%	40,267	96.0%
6,050	98.2%	40,430	96.4%
6,052	98.2%	40,639	96.9%
6,060	98.3%	40,690	97.0%
6,072	98.5%	40,872	97.5%
6,076	98.6%	40,964	97.7%
6,081	98.7%	41,085	98.0%
6,161	**100.0%**	**41,937**	**100.0%**

Rows 11 and 23–51 are not shown, so you can see top, mid-section and bottom-line numbers.

Visualizing a Response Curve

A response curve (Illustration 11.2), derived from the data in the spreadsheet from Illustration 11.1, helps you assess visually how your campaign is performing.

Illustration 11.2

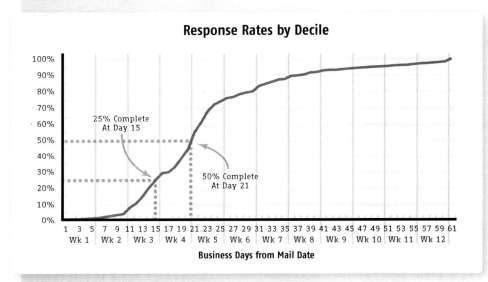

The Hennerberg Analytic Cycle

This flow chart represents the progression and relationships of the principals detailed in this book. The responsible Marketing Portfolio Manager never stops moving through the cycle, continually gathering more data, refining offers, initiating further testing, improving response rates.

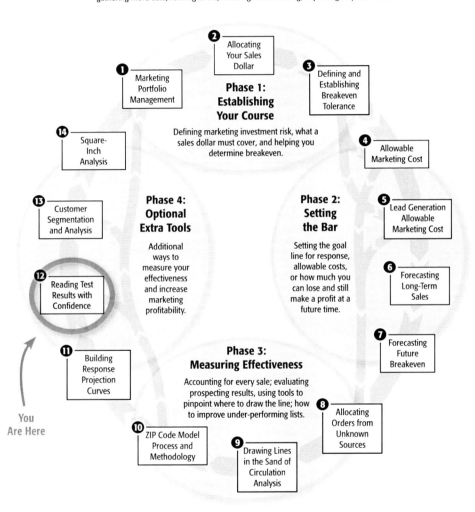

1 Marketing Portfolio Management

2 Allocating Your Sales Dollar

3 Defining and Establishing Breakeven Tolerance

4 Allowable Marketing Cost

5 Lead Generation Allowable Marketing Cost

6 Forecasting Long-Term Sales

7 Forecasting Future Breakeven

8 Allocating Orders from Unknown Sources

9 Drawing Lines in the Sand of Circulation Analysis

10 ZIP Code Model Process and Methodology

11 Building Response Projection Curves

12 Reading Test Results with Confidence

13 Customer Segmentation and Analysis

14 Square-Inch Analysis

Phase 1: Establishing Your Course

Defining marketing investment risk, what a sales dollar must cover, and helping you determine breakeven.

Phase 2: Setting the Bar

Setting the goal line for response, allowable costs, or how much you can lose and still make a profit at a future time.

Phase 3: Measuring Effectiveness

Accounting for every sale; evaluating prospecting results, using tools to pinpoint where to draw the line; how to improve under-performing lists.

Phase 4: Optional Extra Tools

Additional ways to measure your effectiveness and increase marketing profitability.

You Are Here

Chapter 12

Reading Test Results With Confidence

Accurately reading test results from lists, new creative, and offers is vital. A constant quest in direct marketing is to test, refine, and deliver the most profitable direct mail package possible. In creative and offer tests, several direct mail packages (sometimes called kits) are tested against each other in a controlled environment with enough names to read results. Testing is best accomplished when all tests can mail on the same day to randomly selected names from mailing lists.

You should understand how to evaluate one test compared to another.

Testing the right quantity is imperative. If your minimum allowable response rate to meet your profit objective is 1.5 percent (15 orders per thousand) and your test mailing of 5,000 pieces brings 1.75 percent (87 orders), can you be confident your success will be repeated? Unfortunately, the answer is "no."

When you test, you're buying information to help ensure the predictability of future results.

The reason: Statistical probability dictates that future results will fall either on the plus or minus side of past test results. What's more, as a matter of experience, a reconfirming test or rollout usually doesn't outperform the results you experienced in a test.

The possible reasons:

1. **Seasonality** You tested in April, read the results in June and mailed again in July, so you tested during the spring season but mailed again in the summer season.

2. **Time Lapse** Your test offered a brand new product to a brand new market; now competition is creeping up around you. A basic rule is: Your continuation quantity should never exceed 10 times the test. If you test 25,000, then mail no more than 250,000.

3. **Error** You ordered six-month buyers, but the list processor inadvertently sent you 30-day hotline buyers (the best, and most responsive, names), giving you artificially high results.

The exception: If the results are simply phenomenal — double or better than what you expected. At the same time, what if you have experience with the list; you know the list owner to have provided a true, representative sample of prospects; and you feel confident about the entire proposition? In that case, jump on the opportunity immediately.

Why immediately? There is a good chance that the results of the continuation will decline in direct proportion to the amount of time spent preparing the mail to drop again.

Confidence Rates

Think of any test as buying information.

For example, you mailed 5,000 of test package A, and 5,000 of test package B. Package A pulled a 1.75 percent response, and Package B pulled a 2.50 percent response. On the surface, B performed better.

But, if you mailed those two test packages again in the same quantities, would B perform better again? If you want to be confident that 95 out of 100 times B would perform better, the likelihood of that happening again is questionable.

Based on statistical models, 95 out of 100 times B will pull between 2.07 percent and 2.93 percent, and A will pull between 1.39 percent and 2.11 percent. The fact that B could perform as low as 2.07 percent, and A as high as 2.11 percent, suggests there could be mailings where A would pull higher than B. A small quantity like 5,000 names usually is acceptable for list tests (using proven creative and offers), but if you are testing new creative or offers, you should consider higher quantities.

Visualize Response on a Bell Curve

If you seek a 95 percent level of confidence that B will pull higher than A, you'll be disappointed because there is an overlap in projected future response ranges between the two.

It's helpful to visualize the range of response on a bell curve to understand why you can't be confident 95 out of 100 times that B will pull higher than A.

Illustration 12.1, on page 161, shows the distribution of future response 95 percent of the time at the package A test cell response rate of 2.5 percent. In this example, the normal distribution of response in future mailings will be that 47.5 percent of the time response for package A will fall between 2.07 percent and 2.50 percent. Another 47.5 percent of the time,

Future response usually stays within the middle of the bell curve, but sometimes strays to the outer extremes.

response will fall between 2.50 percent and 2.93 percent. Add those two 47.5 percent ranges, and now you have 95 percent of future response between 2.07 and 2.93.

Because it is possible 5 percent of the time that future response will be either above or below that bell curve distribution, 2.5 percent of the time the response could be below 2.07 percent, and 2.5 percent of the time it could be above 2.93 percent.

Contrast Illustration 12.1 with Illustration 12.2, also on page 161. The latter shows the distribution of future response 95 percent of the time at package B's response rate of 1.75 percent. In this example, the normal distribution of response in future mailings will be that 47.5 percent of the time response will fall between 1.39 percent and 1.75 percent. Another 47.5 percent of the time, response will fall between 1.75 percent and 2.11 percent. Add those two 47.5 percent ranges, and now you have 95 percent of future response between 1.39 and 2.11.

Illustration 12.1

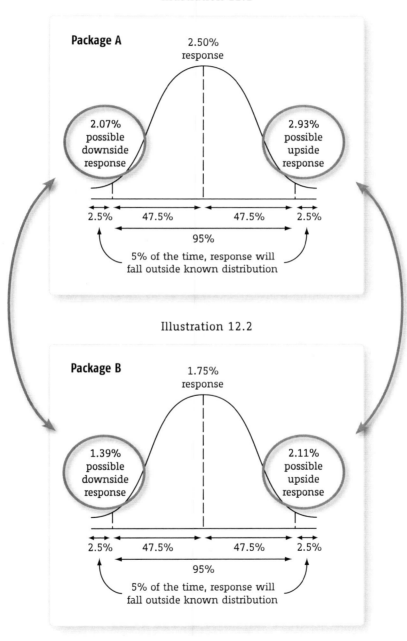

Package A

2.50%
response

2.07%
possible
downside
response

2.93%
possible
upside
response

2.5%   47.5%   47.5%   2.5%

95%

5% of the time, response will
fall outside known distribution

Illustration 12.2

Package B

1.75%
response

1.39%
possible
downside
response

2.11%
possible
upside
response

2.5%   47.5%   47.5%   2.5%

95%

5% of the time, response will
fall outside known distribution

Why demand 95 percent confidence?

Does operating at a 90 percent confidence instead of 95 percent put your business in jeopardy or at other significant financial risk? If 90 percent is okay, is 85 percent acceptable? Or 75 percent (three out of four times — and you mail four times a year)? If you are mailing in high quantities, with considerable sums of marketing investment money on the line, you should want a high confidence factor. But since mailing cost is often a factor in decision making, you may determine that you cannot afford to test in higher quantities that will give you 95 percent confidence.

The Formula to Arrive at These Ranges

You don't have to be a statistical genius to arrive at these response ranges. An understanding of statistics and the relationships between the numbers is advisable, but otherwise you can compute these numbers on a PC or even your calculator (assuming your calculator can tally a square root at the push of a button). Here's the formula in mathematical terms:

Response Rate ("R") = 1.75

Non-Response ("100-R") = 100 − 1.75 = 98.25

Quantity Mailed ("M") = 5,000

$$\text{Standard Error ("SE")} = \sqrt{R \times (100\text{-}R) \ / \ M}$$

$$= \sqrt{(1.75 \times 98.25) \ / \ 5{,}000}$$

$$= \sqrt{171.9375 \ / \ 5{,}000}$$

$$= \sqrt{0.0343875}$$

$$= 0.185439$$

Confidence Level ("C") = 95%
or correct 95 times out of 100
or 1.96 standard errors/
deviations

To be correct 95% of the time, 95 times out of 100:

Confidence Interval ("CI") = SE x C

$$= 0.185439 \text{ x } 1.96$$

$$= 0.0036 \text{ or } 0.36\%$$

Projected response range = R ± CI

$$= 1.75\% \pm 0.36\% \text{ or}$$

$$\text{between } 2.11\% \text{ and } 1.39\%$$

If the mathematical terms aren't resonating with you, try reading this same information in this description:

1. Begin with 100 minus your response percent.

2. Multiply that number by your response percent.

3. Divide that number by your mail quantity.

4. Calculate the square root of that number. What does square root do? The square root of a number backs into the multiplier of itself. For example, the square root of 9 is 3 (3 × 3 = 9), or the square root of 81 is 9 (9 × 9 = 81).

5. If you desire a 95 percent level of confidence, multiply that number by the confidence interval of 1.96, the mathematical factor used for 95 percent confidence.

6. To arrive at your low end of the response range, take your actual response and subtract the number you calculated in step 5.

7. To arrive at your high end of the response range, take your actual response and add the number you calculated in step 5.

Illustration 12.3, next page, offers another way to view the formula.

The formula in conversational terms.

Illustration 12.3

Example "A" at 2.50% Response	Example "B" at 1.75% Response
$(2.5) \times (97.50) \div 5{,}000 = 0.049$	$(1.75) \times (98.25) \div 5{,}000 = 0.034$
$\sqrt{0.049} = 0.220$	$\sqrt{0.034} = 0.185$
$0.220 \times 1.96 = 0.43$	$0.185 \times 1.96 = 0.36$
Low end: $2.50\% - 0.43\% = \mathbf{2.07\%}$	**Low end:** $1.75\% - 0.36\% = \mathbf{1.39\%}$
High end: $2.50\% + 0.43\% = \mathbf{2.93\%}$	**High end:** $1.75\% + 0.36\% = \mathbf{2.11\%}$

Alternate Confidence Levels

As stated earlier, you may not be able to afford a 95 percent level of confidence. To arrive at the 90 percent level of confidence, instead of using 1.96 to determine the confidence interval, use 1.65. For 80 percent confidence, use 1.28. In Illustration 12.4, below, are other statistical factors you might use.

Illustration 12.4

For This Confidence Interval	Use This Number
75%	1.15
80%	1.28
85%	1.44
90%	1.65
95%	1.96
99%	2.58

These factors are based on statistical formulas that calculate confidence levels.

Use Established Benchmarks

If you're an established direct marketer, you already have benchmarks you can use on which to base your test decisions and know if your test package has beaten your control. To be competitive and keep up with changing times, you must keep testing—whether it's a new offer, new creative or new lists. When you've found the new offer, creative execution, or list that performed well in the test, you will want to have an indication of the likely range of response you will receive in the future, especially if you are rolling out from 50,000 to 500,000 names, investing up to 10 times in the rollout what you spent for the test.

If you're testing a new product, it's vital that you identify the winning combination of offers, creative approaches, and lists in a test mode before rolling out. It's often desirable to test several lists, different creative approaches, and offers to identify the magic combination of success, but it is critical that the test matrix be set up so you don't compromise the integrity of statistically predicting your results.

Reminders

You must include enough prospects or customers in your test to obtain reliable results. To find out what's right for you, run assumptions at varying quantities and response levels. The larger the mail quantity, the less variation likely between test and rollout.

A quantity of 5,000 is usually acceptable for a mailing list test, but is not enough to provide reliable creative or offer test results. Depending upon likely response rates and potential rollout quantities, test quantities for new creative could range from 50,000 to 100,000.

An offer or creative test requires 10–20 times as many names as a test of a list to be considered reliable.

While these numbers give you the ranges you'll likely generate, the results from future tests and rollouts will be different if you change the offer, products, or creative. The results also may change, due to factors such as the economy, time of year you mail, or changes in the competitive market.

Using these techniques will help you make a more confident decision for determining which test pulled better and should be rolled out. The numbers will be just one more piece of the puzzle you can use to make your investment decisions for future marketing programs.

The Hennerberg Analytic Cycle

This flow chart represents the progression and relationships of the principals detailed in this book. The responsible Marketing Portfolio Manager never stops moving through the cycle, continually gathering more data, refining offers, initiating further testing, improving response rates.

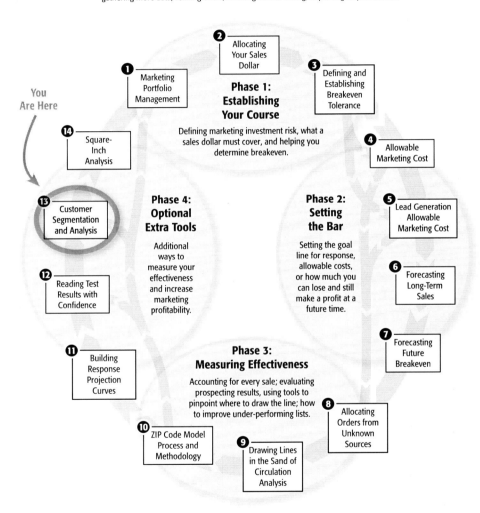

Chapter 13

Customer Segmentation and Analysis

Not all customers are equal. A small percentage of customers probably generate a disproportionately high percentage of your sales. Conversely, a large percentage of customers may generate a low percentage of sales.

You've probably heard of the 80/20 Principle first theorized a century ago by an Italian economist named Vilfredo Pareto. He identified that roughly 80 percent of the wealth went to 20 percent of the people.

The 80/20 ratio is a theory, but the principle is valid for evaluating customer importance.

We know today that there is indeed a predictable imbalance throughout business. It's possible that 20 percent of your customers account for 80 percent of sales and profits, for example. Your opportunity, then, is to perform an analysis to find out if a small percentage of your customers are more valuable to your business than other customers, and act on that information. If you focus on the smaller, but more valuable, percentage of customers, you will likely achieve better profitability.

That's why it's important to develop a process to determine which of your customers are more important to you than others.

An 80/20 ratio is a theory, and you should not expect your organization to have exactly that sales and profit to customer ratio.

In past consumer product analyses I've conducted, one customer ratio identified was 60/40 (60 percent of sales were generated from 40 percent of customers). It was a fairly flat relationship when viewing it across the entire customer database. However, during that analysis the client and I also learned that the top 5 percent of its customers represented 16 percent of its sales. Since this ratio was identified in a database of millions of customers, it prompted the development of a program for only the top 5 percent of customers that was capable of generating more sales.

Extreme ratios: 60/40 from a consumer products marketer; 90/10 from a b-to-b marketer.

On a different extreme, in a business-to-business market another client and I learned that 10 percent of its customers represented 96 percent of its volume. In fact, for a lot of b-to-b companies, the ratio seems to be more 90/10 than 80/20. Upon knowing this ratio, sales people (both field and telephone) were focused on customers who could provide more profit. Customers at the bottom were ignored, because it would cost more money to contact them than it was worth.

So how do you analyze your sales numbers, and what do you do with the data once you've examined it?

Illustration 13.1, on pages 172–173, illustrates how to segment 100 customers. This example gathers the annual purchase value of these 100 customers and sorts the customers from highest to lowest sales (Column B). The percent of total purchases of each customer is calculated in Column D.

Once you have sorted customers from highest to lowest, you can look at the data either by demi-decile (20 equal groups of customers, 5 percent of the customers per group), decile (10 equal groups of customers,

10 percent of the customers per group) or by quintile (five equal groups of customers, 20 percent of the customers per group).

Decile 1, the top 10 percent of customers by number of customers, represents 32.2 percent of sales in this example (F-10). Decile 2, the next group of 10 percent of customers, represents 12.9 percent (F-20), and so on. Decile 10, the last group representing 10 percent of customers, has just 3.2 percent of sales (F-100).

In terms of quintiles, the top quintile (20 percent of customers), represents 45.1 percent of sales (H-20). In contrast, the bottom quintile (the bottom 20 percent of customers) represents 8.2 percent of sales (H-100).

How do you use this information? You might look at it and see that your best 20 percent of customers, who represent 45.1 percent of sales, could be contacted more frequently than other customers. You might develop a customer loyalty program so you don't lose them to a competitor.

At the other end of the spectrum, the bottom 10 percent of customers generates only 3.2 percent of sales. You may choose to curtail marketing to them, or simply not market to them at all. What you gain is a reduction in marketing cost with little exposure to lost sales.

Illustration 13.1

Some rows are not shown, so that summary lines of deciles and quintiles can be displayed.

Line	Customer Annual Purchase	Cumulative Purchases	% of Total Purchases
	A	B	C	D
1	$1,014.16	$1,014.16	5.4%
2	$929.79	$1,943.95	5.0%
9	$333.64	$5,698.60	1.8%
10	$297.65	$5,996.25	1.6%
11	$261.62	$6,257.86	1.4%
19	$226.36	$8,186.28	1.2%
20	$217.51	$8,403.78	1.2%
29	$186.81	$10,184.45	1.0%
30	$183.92	$10,368.37	1.0%
31	$181.77	$10,550.14	1.0%
39	$163.40	$11,917.03	0.9%
40	$161.20	$12,078.23	0.9%
41	$159.33	$12,237.57	0.9%
49	$143.31	$13,434.55	0.8%
50	$141.60	$13,576.15	0.8%
51	$139.31	$13,715.46	0.7%
59	$126.77	$14,771.93	0.7%
60	$124.88	$14,896.81	0.7%
61	$123.58	$15,020.39	0.7%
69	$112.53	$15,958.16	0.6%
70	$111.05	$16,069.21	0.6%
71	$109.82	$16,179.03	0.6%
79	$99.42	$17,007.75	0.5%
80	$98.31	$17,106.07	0.5%
81	$97.24	$17,203.31	0.5%
89	$88.79	$17,943.10	0.5%
90	$87.86	$18,030.96	0.5%
91	$82.33	$18,113.29	0.4%
99	$43.21	$18,591.36	0.2%
100	$38.88	$18,630.24	0.2%
101	$18,630.24		

E	F	G	H
Dollars by Decile (Groups of 10%)	**% Sales by Decile**	**Dollars by Quintile (Groups of 20%)**	**% Sales by Quintile**
~~			
$5,996.25	32.2%		
~~			
$2,407.53	12.9%	$8,403.78	45.1%
$1,964.58	10.5%		
~~			
$1,709.87	9.2%	$3,674.45	19.7%
~~			
$1,497.91	8.0%		
~~			
$1,320.67	7.1%	$2,818.58	15.1%
~~			
$1,172.40	6.3%		
~~			
$1,036.86	5.6%	$2,209.26	11.9%
~~			
$924.89	5.0%		
~~			
$599.28	3.2%	$1,524.17	8.2%
$18,630.24	100.0%	$18,630.24	100.0%

Visualizing the Importance of Certain Customers

Charts are another way to visualize the importance of certain customers. Dollar sales by decile are illustrated in the accompanying bar chart (Illustration 13.2), and percent of sales by decile are illustrated in the pie chart (Illustration 13.3).

Illustration 13.2

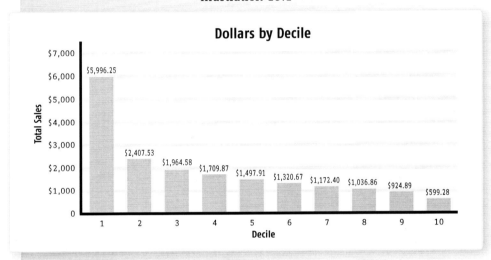

Dollars by Decile

Illustration 13.3

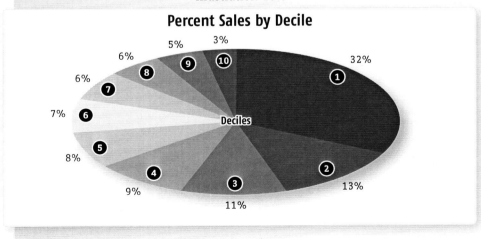

Percent Sales by Decile

The Hennerberg Analytic Cycle

This flow chart represents the progression and relationships of the principals detailed in this book. The responsible Marketing Portfolio Manager never stops moving through the cycle, continually gathering more data, refining offers, initiating further testing, improving response rates.

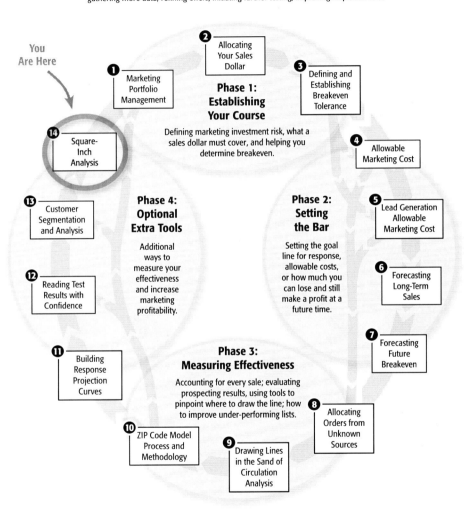

You Are Here

❶ Marketing Portfolio Management

❷ Allocating Your Sales Dollar

❸ Defining and Establishing Breakeven Tolerance

Phase 1: Establishing Your Course

Defining marketing investment risk, what a sales dollar must cover, and helping you determine breakeven.

❹ Allowable Marketing Cost

⓮ Square-Inch Analysis

⓭ Customer Segmentation and Analysis

Phase 4: Optional Extra Tools

Additional ways to measure your effectiveness and increase marketing profitability.

Phase 2: Setting the Bar

Setting the goal line for response, allowable costs, or how much you can lose and still make a profit at a future time.

❺ Lead Generation Allowable Marketing Cost

❻ Forecasting Long-Term Sales

⓬ Reading Test Results with Confidence

❼ Forecasting Future Breakeven

⓫ Building Response Projection Curves

Phase 3: Measuring Effectiveness

Accounting for every sale; evaluating prospecting results, using tools to pinpoint where to draw the line; how to improve under-performing lists.

❽ Allocating Orders from Unknown Sources

❿ ZIP Code Model Process and Methodology

❾ Drawing Lines in the Sand of Circulation Analysis

Chapter 14

Square-Inch Analysis

If you're a catalog marketer, or even if you sell multiple products in a large brochure, one of the key analytic tools at your disposal is the square-inch analysis. This analysis will reveal how each product, and the space it occupies on a catalog's printed page, is performing, relative to the other products/pages. It will tell you to which products you should consider devoting more space. It will give you guidance on how to allocate space for new products. And importantly, it will reveal for what products you should either shrink space allocation, or consider dropping the products entirely from your catalog.

Square-inch analysis will drive your catalog's future pagination and profitability.

You will need to assemble several pieces of information to perform this analysis:

1. Units sold by product.
2. Sales by product, including allocated shipping and handling (S&H) income per product.
3. Square inches of space on a page allocated to each product.
4. Square inches of space used for non-product specific selling purposes.
5. COGS and fulfillment per item, or stated as a percentage of sales.
6. Catalog marketing cost, including photography, design, copy, list rental, pre-press, printing, bindery, postage, and any other related marketing expense.

Overhead allocation is optional, since most catalogers mail several versions of the same catalog over the course of a year.

Here are step-by-step instructions for this analysis for each column of data (also shown in Illustration 14.1, on pages 180–181):

A. Line number

B. Product number

C. Product name or description

D. Page where the product appeared

E. Square inches allocated for the item

F. Units sold

G. Sales. If you charge S&H and plan to include fulfillment as a cost, you should include S&H in sales, either per item or on a weighted average basis.

H. Marketing cost

I. COGS and fulfillment. You will likely want to state this as a percentage of sales, but if you have widely varying costs for each item, you should calculate those costs on a per-item basis.

J. Contribution to Overhead and Profit. Sales less marketing cost, COGS and fulfillment.

K. Contribution to Overhead and Profit per Square Inch. Divide total Contribution by the total number of square inches in the catalog.

L. Sales per Square Inch. Divide sales by the total number of square inches in the entire catalog.

Calculating Square Inches

To calculate square inches for each item, first determine the total square inches on a page. If your catalog is 8⅜" x 10⅞", for example, the actual total square inches on the page is 91.078. You might want to round it to 90 to keep your calculations easier to grasp. An item occupying 75 percent of the page would get 67.5 square inches; 50 percent of the page would get 45 square inches, and so on. For unusual layouts, you may need to use a ruler to measure the space. Be sure the total square inches for items on the page add up to the total you designate for the page (in this example, 90 square inches).

Calculating Marketing Cost

Combine all the costs listed above and divide that cost by the total square inches of selling space. For the example in Illustration 14.1, the cost was calculated as being $450 per square inch for selling space with 84 square inches. This assumes an 8⅜" x 10" size page (83.75 square inches, rounded to 84 square inches per page). In this example, the total marketing cost for this catalog was $1,272,600 (H-76). There were 2,828 square inches of selling space (E-76) so the cost per square inch was $450. For each item, the marketing cost was determined by multiplying $450 by the number of square inches allocated to it.

Sorting data on a square-inch basis will reveal a lot about your merchandise appeal to customers.

You should sort this data in two ways: by sales per square inch and by contribution per square inch. The reason is simply this: If you have high contribution but low sales for an individual item, you may want to reexamine your selling price. A decrease might stimulate sales. Conversely, if you have high sales, but low contribution per square inch, the indicated action is to consider a reduction of selling space.

Illustration 14.1

Line	Product No.	Description	Page No.	Square Inches	Units Sold	Sales
	A	B	C	D	E	F	G
1				28	5,996	$100,927
2				42	4,769	$137,861
3				168	16,167	$541,748
4				84	5,712	$226,512
5				84	6,293	$208,250
6				42	3,639	$103,951
7				42	3,037	$88,001
8				42	3,056	$87,865
9				42	1,868	$84,472
10				42	2,945	$83,840
26				42	1,354	$46,139
27				21	668	$22,857
28				84	2,990	$91,354
29				10.5	145	$11,335
30				42	1,511	$43,274
31				42	1,263	$41,625
32				42	1,450	$41,466
33				42	1,339	$37,993
34				21	524	$17,954
35				42	1,022	$34,770
70				12.6	15	$252
71				12.6	10	$168
72				12.6	9	$151
73				12.6	7	$118
74				12.6	4	$67
75				12.6	2	$40
76				2,828		$3,560,542
77						
79		Back Cover		28		
80		Front Cover		84		
81		Unallocated		420		
82		Total Sq. Inches		3,360		
83		Total Pages		40		

Some rows are not shown, so you can see top, mid-section, and bottom-line numbers.

H	I	J	K	L
Mktg Cost (@ $450/ Sq. In.)	COGS & Flflmnt (56%)	Contrib to OH & Profit	Contrib to OH & Profit per Sq. In.	Sales/ Sq. In.
$12,600	$56,519	$31,808	$1,135.99	$3,604.52
$18,900	$77,202	$41,759	$994.26	$3,282.41
$75,600	$303,379	$162,769	$968.86	$3,224.69
$37,800	$126,847	$61,865	$736.49	$2,696.57
$37,800	$116,620	$53,830	$640.83	$2,479.16
$18,900	$58,212	$26,838	$639.01	$2,475.02
$18,900	$49,281	$19,821	$471.92	$2,095.27
$18,900	$49,204	$19,761	$470.49	$2,092.02
$18,900	$47,304	$18,268	$434.94	$2,011.24
$18,900	$46,951	$17,990	$428.33	$1,996.20
$18,900	$25,838	$1,401	$33.36	$1,098.55
$9,450	$12,800	$607	$28.90	$1,088.41
$37,800	$51,158	$2,396	$28.52	$1,087.54
$4,725	$6,348	$263	$25.01	$1,079.56
$18,900	$24,233	$140	$3.34	$1,030.33
$18,900	$23,310	$(585)	$(13.93)	$991.06
$18,900	$23,221	$(655)	$(15.60)	$987.27
$18,900	$21,276	$(2,183)	$(51.98)	$904.59
$9,450	$10,054	$(1,550)	$(73.83)	$854.93
$18,900	$19,471	$(3,601)	$(85.74)	$827.86
$5,670	$141	$(5,559)	$(441.18)	$20.04
$5,670	$94	$(5,596)	$444.12)	$13.36
$5,670	$85	$(5,603)	$(444.71)	$12.02
$5,670	$66	$(5,618)	$(445.89)	$9.35
$5,670	$38	$(5,640)	$(447.65)	$5.34
$5,670	$23	$(5,652)	$(448.59)	$3.21
$1,272,600	$1,993,904	$294,038	$103.97	$1,259.03

You can define your own parameters, for both sales and contribution, into three ratings: high, acceptable, and low. In other words, you need to decide what dollar threshold you would define as, say, "high sales per square inch." You also need to define at what point sales per square inch slides into the "low" category. The numbers in between can be characterized as "acceptable."

You'll need to perform the same exercise for contribution and define "high," "acceptable," and "low." Using Illustration 14.2, you can determine how to adjust your space allocation for your next catalog. Of course, this sample matrix is intended to be directional only. You'll need to make adjustments for your own situation.

Illustration 14.2

	Low Sales per Sq. In.	Acceptable Sales/Sq. In.	High Sales per Sq. In.
High Contribution per Square Inch	Maintain or increase space	Maintain or increase space	Maintain or increase space
Acceptable Contribution per Square Inch	Maintain or increase space	Reduce space	Maintain or reduce space
Low Contribution per Square Inch	Consider dropping the item	Reduce space	Reduce space

The Hennerberg Analytic Cycle

This flow chart represents the progression and relationships of the principals detailed in this book. The responsible Marketing Portfolio Manager never stops moving through the cycle, continually gathering more data, refining offers, initiating further testing, improving response rates.

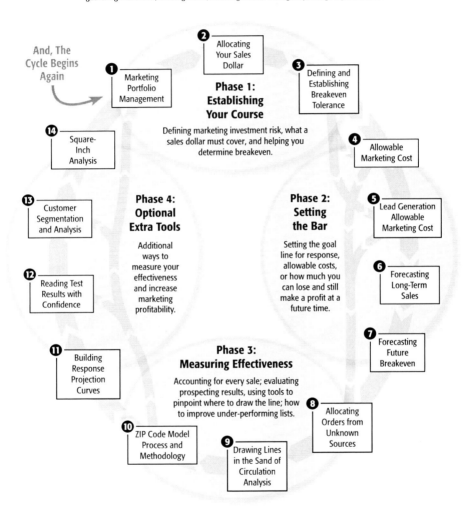

And, The Cycle Begins Again

❶ Marketing Portfolio Management

❷ Allocating Your Sales Dollar

❸ Defining and Establishing Breakeven Tolerance

Phase 1: Establishing Your Course

Defining marketing investment risk, what a sales dollar must cover, and helping you determine breakeven.

❹ Allowable Marketing Cost

❺ Lead Generation Allowable Marketing Cost

❻ Forecasting Long-Term Sales

❼ Forecasting Future Breakeven

Phase 2: Setting the Bar

Setting the goal line for response, allowable costs, or how much you can lose and still make a profit at a future time.

❽ Allocating Orders from Unknown Sources

Phase 3: Measuring Effectiveness

Accounting for every sale; evaluating prospecting results, using tools to pinpoint where to draw the line; how to improve under-performing lists.

❾ Drawing Lines in the Sand of Circulation Analysis

❿ ZIP Code Model Process and Methodology

⓫ Building Response Projection Curves

Phase 4: Optional Extra Tools

Additional ways to measure your effectiveness and increase marketing profitability.

⓬ Reading Test Results with Confidence

⓭ Customer Segmentation and Analysis

⓮ Square-Inch Analysis

Chapter 15

Taking Action

Smart direct marketers know that strategic knowledge is in the numbers. This book has walked you through a step-by-step process cycle to enable you to become more knowledgeable about how to measure the success of your marketing programs.

You now should feel some degree of empowerment when you use these tools and begin to think globally about your role in defining the financial success of your organization. Knowing what every sales dollar must cover and that increased profit comes from decreased marketing cost is fundamental to building a profitable business.

But understanding the details of the numbers, and how to strategically apply them, is where businesses are made or fall into trouble.

I've packed many years of hands-on experience into these pages and models. You shouldn't expect to completely understand everything until you actually have created your own models, tested your theories, and witnessed the live results.

Crunching numbers takes time.

And, if you're attempting to comprehend and apply many or all of these techniques and models to your situation for the first time, it's a mind-bending exercise.

Whether you run the numbers yourself, assign someone on your internal team to be your numbers guru, or retain outside help, marketing analysis needs to be performed. An audit performed by an impartial outside expert will remove the emotional attachment to a set of beliefs or other preconceived ideas.

The knowledge for profitably managing your direct marketing business truly is in the numbers. Use the numbers strategically. Apply them wisely. And greater profit is sure follow.

Direct Marketing Analytic and Creative Consulting Services

Do you agree that the knowledge is in the numbers, but would like to team with a qualified expert to take on the task of gathering and analyzing the data, and making recommendations? We have over 25 years of experience developing long-term value, breakeven, circulation analysis, ZIP modeling, and more—everything you've read in this book—for organizations in a variety of industries.

In addition, Hennerberg Group, Inc. specializes in turnkey direct mail advertising agency solutions. Our consulting services encompass analytics and creative work, including copywriting and direct mail design. We are a direct marketing services firm that understands how to effectively blend the direct marketing synergy pyramid—lists, offer, and creative—to maximize your advertising and marketing success.

Our goal is not to win creativity awards, but rather for *you* to win by generating greater profits through marketing and advertising that effectively sells.

We provide end-to-end direct marketing advertising services. We manage copywriting, design, list acquisition, production, and more. In direct mail creative tests we've outperformed control packages by over 60% on multiple occasions.

Contact us for strategy and creative, production management, or in-house training and seminars, and let us fire up your direct marketing program.

Learn more at hennerberg.com

HENNERBERG GROUP, INC.